Kitchens

Kitchens
A design sourcebook

Vinny Lee

with photography by
James Merrell

RYLAND
PETERS
& SMALL

LONDON NEW YORK

Art Director **Jacqui Small**

Senior Designer **Penny Stock**

Senior Editor **Sian Parkhouse**

Assistant Designer **Stuart Edwards**

Editorial Assistant **Maddalena Bastianelli**

Production Manager **Meryl Silbert**

Location Researcher **Nadine Bazar**

Stylist **Cynthia Inions**

Dedication
To AWJ, my companion in life's steamy kitchen

First published in the USA in 1998
This updated edition published in 2001 by
by Ryland Peters & Small, Inc.,
519 Broadway, 5th Floor
New York NY 10012
www.rylandpeters.com

Text © Vinny Lee 1998, 2001
Design and photographs © Ryland Peters & Small 1998

ISBN 1-84172-227-8

Printed and bound in China.

10 9 8 7 6 5 4 3 2 1

contents

introduction

The role of the kitchen has changed dramatically in the last twenty or thirty years, from being a purely functional place to one that is an integral part of the home. These days the kitchen has to fulfill many roles, from preparing and storing food to that of a laundry and, in some cases, a dining or family room as well. Numerous other demands are made on this space, from supplying the household with the most basic and old-fashioned needs of fire and water to having the technological requirements necessary for the installation of increasingly sophisticated labor-saving machines and gadgets.

Our changing lifestyles influence what we expect of this room: for example, space for bigger refrigerators and freezers to store more food so that the once daily stop at the local market can be reduced to a weekly supermarket run. More things are kept in the fridge; not just fresh perishable dairy foods but also fruit, vegetables, preserves, and soft drinks—many things that previously would have been stored in a pantry or larder.

Cooking itself has become more than just the supply of sustenance. Recipes, ingredients, and styles of cooking from around the world have hugely increased the home cooks' repertoire in recent time. Woks, steamers, rice cookers, ice-cream machines, and pasta makers are now found in households far beyond their native countries. Preprepared and "instant" foods have become increasingly popular with teenagers and in busy working households. These foods have caused the microwave to become the mainstay of numerous kitchens, and, in some cases, the alternative to a conventional stove.

In many countries the kitchen is now the center of home life and domestic activity. The demise of the traditional formal dining room has seen the kitchen become a living and eating area, so the design and decoration of the kitchen has become more important. Modern homes are also turning to open-plan design, where there is little or no definition or segregation of the different parts of the living areas. In the main, the kitchen is no longer the solely functional space it once was—it now features predominately in the overall planning and decoration of a home.

The development of new laminates and materials has also seen the kitchen become a more colorful and fashionable room. No longer restricted to the limitations imposed by practical wipe-clean ceramic tiles and gloss paint-work, the kitchen can now be decorated with specially finished rustproof metals; reinforced, sandblasted, and etched glass; colored woods; and durable plastic. New seals and finishes mean that more traditional materials, such as slate and wood, can be made more resilient to the wear and tear and extremes of daily kitchen life.

Kitchen styles, like clothes fashions, now come from a whole range of sources, from the colorful richness of cheerful rustic Mediterranean farm-houses to the high-tech streamlined designs of steel-clad professional kitchens. Nostalgia is a perennial influence: period styles, such as Victorian, 1950s, or Colonial, are all sources of inspiration for kitchen designs and are frequently adapted to suit the plans, requirements, and modern gadgetry of the contemporary kitchen.

Left A kitchen may be part of an open-plan space that includes living and dining functions, in which case the layout and design of the kitchen will be an integral part of the whole room scheme.

Below **Tried and tested utensils never go out of date. A good size, sturdy wooden chopping board and a robust enamel jug are classics that still find their place in the modern kitchen.**
Right **Keeping all the storage elements of this kitchen at a low level makes the linear layout appear spacious and uncluttered, and gives the room the appearance of height.**

So, whether you are designing a kitchen from scratch, renovating an old one, or replanning an existing one, it is wise to prepare yourself—to be sure in your own mind about what you want. But also be open to the advice offered by the professionals, especially in technical areas such as installation, wiring, and plumbing. Reading and researching about kitchens will help you accumulate the information you need to make important decisions that could, in the end, affect your daily routine and the smooth running of your life.

Building or altering a kitchen is a project that requires careful planning and execution, as it is invariably a labor-intensive and costly exercise. Updating a scheme can be as simple as buying new accessories or changing unit doors, but if you are undertaking extensive changes or the installation of a new kitchen there are many questions to answer and aspects to consider before embarking on the project. If you are working to a strict budget it is also wise to be aware of the added extras and the unexpected costs that may arise so that you

can plan a contingency fund to cover such incidental expenses. All of these points and more, such as the practical, safety, and hygiene standards and requirements, have to be considered, while still creating a room that is attractive and comfortable for those who work and/or eat there.

Technical advancements in kitchen equipment are constant and fast moving, so it is worthwhile spending some time browsing around major kitchen appliance shops or department stores to check out what is new and to consider the options. There are fashions in gadgets and machines—the trendiest ones may instantly appeal, but soon find their way into the obsolete or rarely used drawer or quickly become dated. Beware of this when you are shopping around—consider longevity and durability when purchasing.

Also, do not be overwhelmed by fashionable styles in kitchens—think of the practicalities. Some of the high-tech professional-style kitchens are fine if you have a battery of *sous* chefs and staff to scrub down the surfaces and clean the place from top to bottom each day, but if you are on your own, keeping the shining steel surfaces immaculately clean can be a overwhelming task. Also, in practical terms, some of the larger industrial ranges have large pan supports designed to take commercial-size pots and pan, and an omelette pan designed for one person will fall through the gaps. Even the more traditional-style kitchens, with pots and pans hanging from beams or rafters, are prone to the accumulation of grease and odd splashes of fat and boiling sauces; so hang pots and pans if you wish, but do so away from work surfaces where frying and cooking take place to cut down on time spent on cleaning.

When embarking on planning or redesigning a kitchen, it is absolutely vital to be ruthlessly honest with yourself, and to fit a kitchen that suits your lifestyle in addition to your style aspirations. But above all, make sure the kitchen you end up with is one where you feel at home. It should be a place that is comfortable and practical to work in, but also a place where your friends feel welcome to come and chat while you cook, to drink coffee, and to gossip. The kitchen is no longer a place of toil and labor— it is often the most sociable and used room in a home, so it should be one that can be enjoyed on many levels.

nciples

planning and design

fitting and installing

introduction

When you have decided that you need a new kitchen or that your existing one needs updating, where and how do you start? Don't rush in thinking that a few cabinets and a couple of appliances will suffice, they won't—it takes time and effort to create a well-designed, practical layout. A kitchen is a functional space and one that requires a certain amount of financial commitment. Expenditure is needed for both materials and equipment, but it is money that, well spent, will be an investment for years to come.

A good kitchen is said to add value to a property, but it is the room that a new purchaser will most often change, whether cosmetically with new paint and tiles or dramatically with a replan and new units. The size of investment you make in your kitchen will depend on whether you plan to stay in the home for a considerable period or whether it is a short-term residence. A kitchen in the second category will need to be a good, safe workplace, but it should be decorated in neutral or low-key colors and with fixtures that are classic rather than too fashionable or idiosyncratic, so that they will encourage rather than put off a potential purchaser.

Planning is the most important part of installing a kitchen. Spending time and effort on this initial stage will save headaches later on. Working with an architect or professional kitchen planner can make the task easier, but it is important to know what you want and to be aware of the vast range of products and finishes available. No one expects you to become an instant expert, but the more groundwork and research you do, the more options you give yourself. Whether the kitchen is built in or freestanding, the three basic requirements are a heat source, a supply of water, and cold storage. Around these you can add storage for food, china, and flat-ware; counters on which to prepare food; then the electrical and plumbing needs such as waste disposal, a dishwasher, sockets, lighting, and so on. Once these have been allocated a position and the basic functioning of the kitchen worked out, then the "dressings"—the colors and finishes—can be planned and discussed.

Think of the process like the structure of a car. The form and function of the kitchen is like the engine—this has to be fine-tuned before the outer layers are added. If the engine is badly adjusted then no matter how fine and expensive the dressings are, the car will fail to function properly. With the elements of fire and water operating in the kitchen there are inherent dangers, so good installation is vital to avoid accidents.

Opposite Smooth, unobstrusive lines and well-planned preparation and storage areas are essential in a practical working kitchen. Getting the basics right is the key to a successful result.

planning
and design

The first and most important thing to get clear in your mind is what you want from your kitchen. Define the purpose of the space and how often it will be used. Look at your lifestyle and circumstances. Do you live alone? Are you a professional couple without children? Or are you a family with children? And how many people will be using the kitchen on a regular basis?

Next, gauge how often it will be used and how much storage space will be needed. The questions that will help you get these answers are: Do you enjoy cooking and entertaining or do you tend to buy prepared foods or eat out a lot? If you entertain, how many people do you have on average—mainly small suppers for four to six or grand dinners for ten to twelve? Do you usually shop daily, weekly, or monthly? Is food storage mainly for fresh produce or for frozen and canned goods? This will give you an idea of how much dry or shelf storage you should allow for and how big a refrigerator you might need.

It is important to have an accurate idea of the expected usage of the kitchen. For example, an urban-dwelling, busy professional couple who have the occasional pasta or preprepared meal at home will not need the same size kitchen or as much storage space as the family with three small children who live in the country and eat most meals at home. Is the area to be used solely for food preparation and cooking or is the kitchen area part of a room with another purpose? For example, will the space be used for family and friends to sit around and talk, watch television, and relax? Is the kitchen also a laundry area, with a washing machine and drier installed?

Assess the dimensions and the pros and cons of the area. This will give you a clear understanding of the layout and disadvantages and advantages of the space. How many doors are there? Do they open in or out, and are all of them needed? Are there any unusual pillars or other features that cause the walls to be irregular rather than flat? If the room is small, can other functions,

Opposite **When planning a kitchen aim is to create a welcoming place.**
Above **Consider many different types of storage for versatility.**
Top right **A table top provides multi-purpose work and dining space.**
Right **The kitchen must be functioning as well as look good: it will not remain immaculate!**

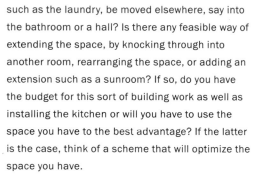

such as the laundry, be moved elsewhere, say into the bathroom or a hall? Is there any feasible way of extending the space, by knocking through into another room, rearranging the space, or adding an extension such as a sunroom? If so, do you have the budget for this sort of building work as well as installing the kitchen or will you have to use the space you have to the best advantage? If the latter is the case, think of a scheme that will optimize the space you have.

When planning a small kitchen draw inspiration from similar-size areas, such as a ship's galley or a trailer or mobile home. In these situations the wall space is utilized with half shelves built under overhead cupboards, but still giving full access to the counter. Overhead hanging rods, from which utensils can be hung, are also space saving, but make sure they are positioned in a place where you are not likely to bump into them, ideally over a stove or a central unit.

Finally, look around and see how much natural light there is in the room. If there is little or none, consider ways of obtaining or increasing the amount of daylight by installing a roof skylight or french doors. Also look to see if there is access to outside walls for ducting. This is particularly important in apartments, where kitchens may be sited in the interior of the building. Machines such as exhaust fans and tumble driers need an outer wall for their ducts. This can, in some cases, be done

through other methods, but they may be expensive to install and be obtrusive. Locate the waste outlets and water pipes also, which will indicate where major plumbing, such as the sink and dishwasher, should be installed if possible.

Making a plan

When you have drawn up a comprehensive list of all the functions that will take place in the room, it is time to start manipulating the space available to accommodate them. The easiest way to do this is to draw an accurate scale outline of the kitchen on graph paper. Installing a kitchen is a serious and permanent investment, so it is worth taking time to try various plans before deciding on the final layout. The paper plan is the easiest way to try different combinations on your own, but if you have access to a computer and suitable software a design program is the quickest way to generate detailed plans very quickly. You could also discuss your ideas with a professional kitchen planner, and some kitchen manufacturers may be able to show you layouts similar to the ones you are considering in their own showrooms. It can be very difficult to visualize how cabinets, colors, and plans will look in reality and it is hard to predict and accommodate every mistake or oversight that may occur in the installation stage, but try to preempt as much as you can since it will, in the long term, save you time and money.

Top left **Storage space is important. A plate rack can be used to hold china as well as allow it to drip dry over a draining board or sink.**
Top center **Smaller items of foodstuffs and utensils can get lost on open shelving so store them in larger containers that are attractive enough to put on display: a wicker basket is ideal for keeping vegetables because air circulates through it.**
Top right **Items used frequently should be stored close to hand so that you do not have to waste time searching for them.**
Above and opposite **Basic open shelves provide good storage because items are easily seen and can be immediately identified.**

A wall of superbly crafted cupboards conceals all the paraphernalia of the kitchen—from china and glass to refrigerators and comestibles. When closed the cupboards appear to be a paneled wall, but behind this façade is well-planned and spacious storage. This type of arrangement is ideal in a kitchen/dining area where formal entertaining takes place.

Top left and left **A checkerboard effect achieved
with two shades of tile brings a touch of pattern
into an otherwise plain setting. It creates a visual
division between cooking and sitting/eating areas.**
Top center **A spray attachment on a long flexible
hose and a faucet with an adjustable spout means
that water can be directed exactly where it is
needed, which makes cleaning vegetables and
washing pans a simpler task.**
Top right and above **This upright integral sink has a
built-in backsplash and takes up less space than a
traditional sink.**
Opposite **The kitchen area is an integral part of this
open-plan living and dining room. The decoration,
which has been kept the same throughout, is
clean and simple, but not dull. Interest has been
added by the use of a two-tone covering on the
façade of the kitchen's corner unit and in the
choice of interesting furniture and lighting.**

Plot in the general shape of the room on your paper or computer plan, and then add features such as windows, doors, hot and cold water pipes, electrical outets, and radiators (although these can be moved, it is worth putting them in to give yourself an idea of where plumbing and electrical costs may occur). Try to keep windows free of overhead cabinets or anything that may block the light. In front of a window is a good place to have a chopping board or a counter so food preparation can be carried out in maximum light. When you are marking in where the doors and windows are note how they open, as this may affect access to cabinets. For example, if the room door opens flat against a cupboard door, it may be difficult to get into the cupboard.

Choosing appliances

If you have existing appliances or furniture that will be used again, draw the items to scale on another piece of paper, then cut them out and label them. Do the same for any new pieces of equipment you are thinking of buying. This is the time to think carefully about the size and capacity of the machines you

want to buy. If you use your refrigerator for storing most of your food, you can probably sacrifice dry or shelf storage space to accommodate a big fridge, but if you only keep salad vegetables and milk in the refrigerator, allow more shelf and cupboard space for canned or packaged foods.

If you live alone, eat breakfast on the way to work, and only have a couple of friends over once a month for a bowl of soup and a cheese sandwich, then a dishwasher with a twenty place-setting capacity is not for you. What you probably want is a small machine with six place-settings that can be run through twice to cope with a busy evening. Is a twin sink and double drainer necessary if you have a dishwasher? Would a single sink and one drainer suffice?

Similar analysis should also be used when you buy a stove. If you do not like cooking, do you need an oven. Would burners and a microwave cover your requirements? The six-ring, double-oven industrial stove may look wonderful in the showroom and in magazine articles, but in reality will you use all six rings and both ovens or would a smaller version be more practical? Find out the dimensions of the equipment you are planning to buy and again make scale

Left **The surfaces near the stove or burners should, ideally, be heat resistant so that hot plates or pots can be put down quickly and easily when they are being taken out of the oven or removed from the heat of a burner.**

Below **Steel is a good heat-resistant surface but it also makes an excellent general counter surface. It can be quickly cooled down with cold water or ice, which makes it, like marble, useful for piecrust preparation. Usually seam free, steel is also easy to wipe clean and devoid of ridges and niches where grime might collect.**

drawings. Place the cutouts of all the equipment and furniture on the floor plan and try to make them fit. You may find that you need to compromise and opt for a smaller appliance or a different configuration. For example, you may find that the double oven you wanted is too big for the area you have and that a wall-mounted oven and separate burners would be better. Or that the stove can be accommodated, but the refrigerator-freezer will have to be two separate smaller units placed side by side. When you are trying this manipulation of space and machines, keep a list of alternative equipment to refer to, with designs and sizes that provide a similar capacity or function.

The work triangle

A rule of thumb to planning a kitchen is to use what is known as the work triangle. The theory is that the main work areas—the sink, the stove, and the refrigerator—should be sited so they form an imaginary triangle. This provides the most efficient use of space and time. For example, in the course of the preparation of a meal, you would get the ingredients from the refrigerator, take them to the sink to wash them, and then turn to the oven to cook them, so in an ideal plan these three work stations should be within easy reach of each other. It is also worth taking into consideration where the main flow of traffic through the kitchen will be. Ideally the work triangle should not be in the middle of this area as accidents may occur when people cross through. The area

where people come to or from a table or eating area should also be away from the oven. Consider also the inclusion of counter space on either side of the stove so hot or heavy dishes can be put down quickly and safely. Keep machines of similar function together, for example, the washing machine next to the drier and the dishwasher near the sink for easy plumbing, but also near cupboards where everyday china, glass, and flatware are stored—this will cut down on the amount of lifting and carrying that has to be done.

As a general rule there should be a panel between a refrigerator-freezer and stove to prevent the heat from the stove affecting the efficiency of the fridge, although most modern refrigerators are now well insulated. Also allow plenty of space for appliance doors to open. Dishwasher doors that generally open from top to bottom require more room because you have to stand in front or to the side of the door to fill and empty the machine; the same applies to front-loading washing machines. Refrigerator or cupboard doors that open right to left may not need to be opened right back, so they take up less space.

Built in or not?

Once the machines and equipment are in place on your plan, you can start filling in the remaining areas with storage space and counters. At this point you have to address the question of whether a built-in kitchen is the best option. This is also a matter of taste: some people prefer the tailored lines of a built-in

Left If you are planning to place a refrigerator-freezer directly next to a powerful stove, check with the manufacturers or suppliers of both appliances that the refrigerator mechanism will not be affected by the heat that is output by the stove or the burners. If there is likely to be a problem, installing a heatproof insulation panel between the refrigerator and the stove will help prevent defrosting or damage to the refrigerator exterior.
Below left Having a rim or resting area around the edge of burners or a broiler is useful for putting down dripping or hot spoons or utensils.

kitchen while others opt for the versatility and flexibility of the freestanding variety. In smaller rooms built-in kitchens are often the best option because they can be planned and installed to use every available inch of space. But the advantage of freestanding cabinets is that you can take them with you when you move. This means that it is worth investing in more expensive pieces of furniture because you will get longer use from them. If you are living in temporary housing such as a rented apartment, well-made freestanding cabinets will look good, give you pleasure, and travel with you when you leave your current address. With freestanding furniture you can take your time and gradually build up your kitchen, getting to know the room and your requirements before adding the next unit. It also means that you can spread the cost over months or years instead of having to commit a substantial amount of money at once, as you would when buying a built-in design.

Mixing and matching cabinets can also create an interesting look. Antique hutches alongside a steel-topped workbench will bring together old and new in a way that a preplanned built-in kitchen may not achieve. This sort of arrangement is also versatile—for example, if a hutch or chest is no longer needed in the kitchen, it can be moved to another room and become a linen closet for towels and bedclothes. You can also make a virtue out of having a mix-and-match collection of cabinets. You could opt for a rainbow range of colors rather than trying to conform to a regular or limited scheme. Paint each piece of furniture a different shade of the same color, or with a spectrum of colors, then go the whole way and add different knobs and handles so the eclectic appearance is carried all the way through. A decorative backsplash in a harlequin mix of colored ceramic tiles could complete the bohemian look.

Mobile furniture

In a freestanding kitchen heavier cabinets should ideally be mounted on wheels or castors so they can be easily moved away from the wall for cleaning or redecorating. It is important to make sure the unit is level and sturdy so that it will not teeter or fall over—this is especially important with larger cabinets. If you add castors or wheels, try to use the type that have lever brakes so that the unit can be stabilized when it is in position.

Mobile furniture may also be used to create different settings or emphasis in a room. For example, if you cook and entertain in the same place, a lightweight bookcase with a solid back, filled with a few choice books and pieces of china, might be wheeled in front of a work surface (don't overburden it or it will be heavy and difficult to move). This will create a temporary wall between the cooking and eating areas; then it can be pushed back against the

Right **The reverse side of a cabinet can be used as a display area or bookcase.**
Below right **When installing cabinets, make sure they are at a comfortable height so you do not get backaches from leaning over low counters.**
Opposite **This island sink unit creates a corridor to the right which leads to the far end of the room. Not putting cupboards above the sink keeps the space open, allowing the light from the french doors to penetrate into the kitchen area.**

wall when not needed. Butcher blocks are useful because they can be stored under the counter or in a corner but brought out to provide extra preparation space. Vegetable baskets are similarly adaptable; they can be brought out when shopping is being unpacked and rolled back into their storage area, then taken to the sink for vegetables to be removed for washing and preparation.

For people who spend time in the kitchen and prepare food from scratch, it is important that cabinets and appliances are at the correct height. The function of the kitchen sink is now mainly replaced by the dishwasher, but vegetables and pots and pans, as well as valuable china and delicate crystal glasses, are still washed by hand. Stooping over a low sink or stretching to a high counter can be laborious and is likely to cause accidents, so make sure the base of the sink or height of the counter are at a comfortable level. A mix of mid-height and taller cabinets will make it possible for a couple who are of notably different heights to work without incurring backaches from leaning over or stretching beyond their natural reach. Eye-level broilers should be at eye level—if not it is difficult to watch food being cooked and you may burn your hand on the broiler when the pan is removed. So make sure the kitchen is built to suit *your* height and eye level rather than that of the "average" person.

A multifunction kitchen

If you plan to use your kitchen in different ways, it is best to think of the room divided into sections. Assign an area for cooking and food preparation, another for eating, and a third for sitting and relaxing. Ideally there should be a logical order to the layout so when the food is ready to be eaten it can be quickly and easily transferred to the table in the eating area. The seating area should be farthest away from the food preparation section, so that when the kitchen work is done, it can be cleared and the lights turned off. It is also safer to take hot dishes directly to the eating area instead of walking through a busy living area.

If the room is too small to subdivide into three separate areas, subtract or condense the functions until you can allow comfortable space for each one. For example, an island unit or peninsula without overhead cupboards could double as a eating table with the addition of high stools and still create a division between cooking and seating areas. The eating space that doubles as a living area should have chairs that are comfortable enough to linger in after a meal and a table that is at a good height to do homework or other pastimes. Or a foldaway table and chairs could be used for dining and put away when not in use, and armchairs on castors could be pushed to the outer edges of the room when meals are in progress. Alternatively, the living and dining functions could be combined by having an adjustable table that is raised when you are eating and lowered to coffee-table height when you are relaxing.

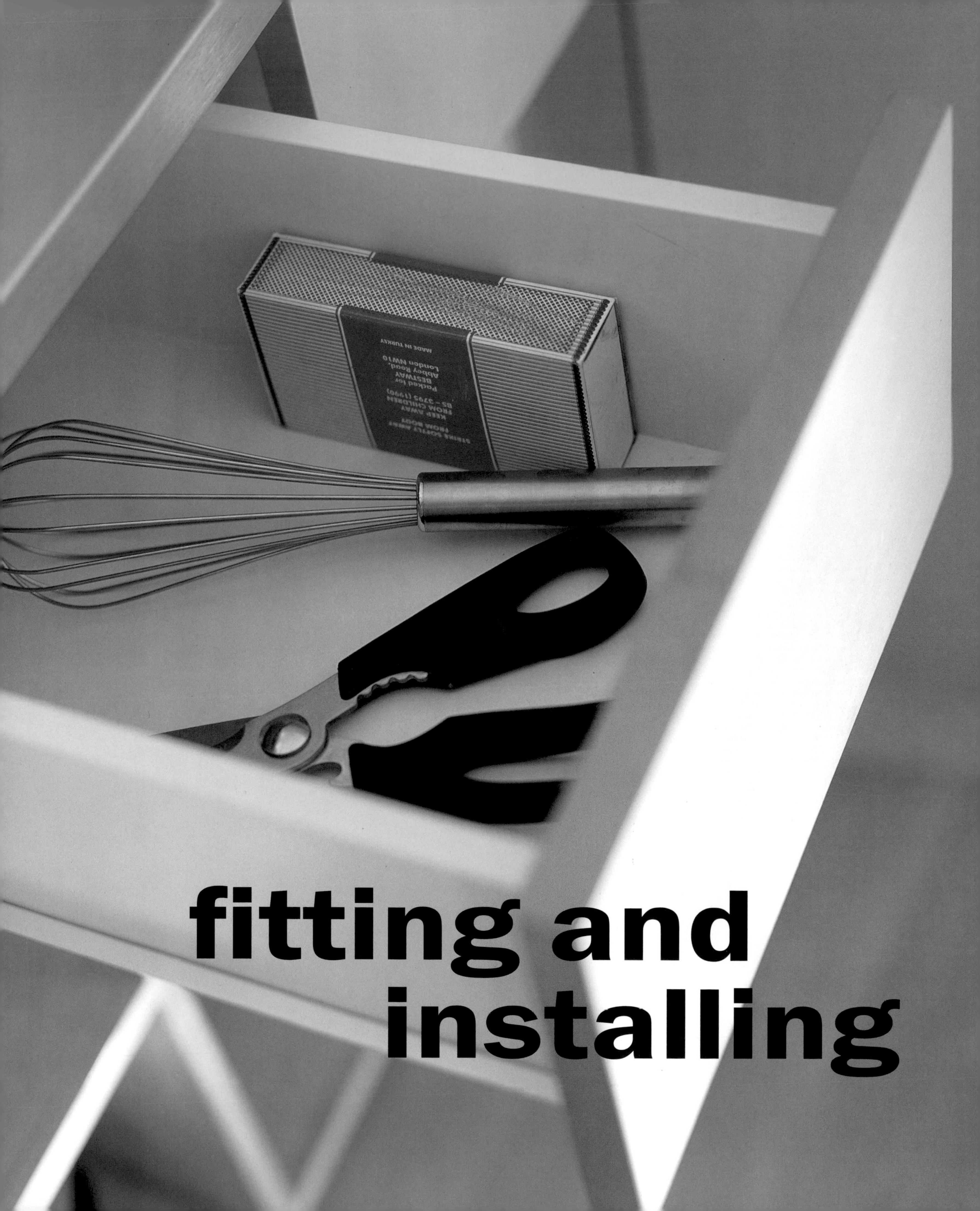
STRIKE SOFTLY AWAY FROM BODY
KEEP AWAY FROM CHILDREN
BS - 3795 (1990)
Packed for BESTWAY Abbey Road, London NW10
MADE IN TURKEY

fitting and installing

Unless you are a very talented and competent builder, the installation of a kitchen is something best left to the professionals, but it is worth knowing the basics and a little about the work involved so you can be prepared for what is to come. Being acquainted with the overall schedule will also help you to have things ready as and when they are needed. For example, finding the right tiles should take preference over a wall-mounted spice rack that will not be hung until after the tiles are in place. Keeping your eyes open and being involved in the installation may also help you notice hitches and problems as they arise so they can be solved while the work is in progress rather than later when the cabinets are secured and tiles and counters are fixed in place.

Once you have more or less decided on your kitchen plan, it is time to gather quotations from builders, plumbers, and electricians to keep a focus on how much it is likely to cost and to make sure you are still within your budget. It is worth getting a couple of quotes so you can compare prices, and if one is far lower or far higher than another, ask why the difference is so radical. The explanation may help you choose one workman above another. Also ask for references—someone who has experience of their work before may provide you with useful information. If you are buying your own cabinets and major appliances check with the installer as to whether he or she can get the items more cheaply. People in the trade can often buy items at wholesale prices and may be prepared to buy the item through a trade-only outlet if they are commissioned to install the item in your home.

If you are arranging your own installation, plan to do it in a logical order. For example, it is best to have electrical wiring, say for recessed ceiling lights and wall sockets, done before any plastering and tiling are in place. It is better to have the cabinets and appliances installed after the floor has been laid so they can rest on top of the flooring rather than have tiles or linoleum butting up to the edge of the unit. If the line fits up to the edge rather than under the unit, it may peel back in time, but the weight of the machine or unit will help anchor the flooring in place. It may also be worth having most of the paintwork done before the cabinets are installed so there is less danger of paint being splashed on them. Although the process of installing cabinets may incur scuffs or scratches, these can be touched up later when the building work is done.

Installing cabinets

Once you have decided on the layout of the kitchen, where the appliances will go, and how the cabinets should be placed, it is time to get down to the basics. If your kitchen is to be custom-made you will have cupboards designed and built to suit your room. With a freestanding kitchen you have more flexibility, but the size and shape of the furniture will still be influenced by the capacity and angles of the kitchen. If you choose a commercially produced, standard

Left **Smooth-running drawers are a sign of a well-built kitchen.**
Top right **An apparently unsupported bench provides extra work surface but does not block out light.**
Right **Adjustable shelving is good in cabinets where you keep lightweight goods. For heavy equipment fixed shelves are a more sturdy option.**

kitchen you will have to consider how the premade cabinets, known as carcasses, can be adapted to suit your needs and the dimensions of your room. Very few kitchens are perfectly symmetrical, and fewer still will be just the right size to accommodate an exact number of prefabricated cupboards, which come in standard sizes. There are two basic types of cabinets used in built-in kitchens—base and wall mounted. Fill-in cabinets such as a tall broom cupboard may also be available as standard, but not all manufacturers supply them. Most mass-produced cupboard carcasses are made from chipboard, plywood, or composition board with a standard melamine finish.

Internally they may have built-in rigid shelves or adjustable ones that can be moved up and down. Other cabinets have a single drawer above a smaller cupboard space or are fitted with a set of drawers. Most cabinets have adjustable legs that can be concealed, when the unit is secured, by kickboard panels at the base of the unit. These cabinets are almost all standard in shape and construction; it is the doors, whether from a stock selection or custom made, that give the kitchen its character and style.

Think carefully about the combination and location of these cabinets so that drawers for flatware and cloths are near the area where they will be needed and the shelves for storage will be in an area where they are accessible. For example, it is usually wise to have a shelf-free cupboard under the sink so you can keep detergents and dishwashing liquids together in that space and

Above **A built-in bench provides more seating space than could be achieved with individual chairs.**
Right **This combination of built-in and freestanding furniture creates an informal but smart appearance.**

away from foodstuffs that might be tainted by scents or soapy flavors. Put heavier pots, pans, and equipment in base cupboards rather than in wall-mounted ones where too much weight may cause the cabinet to come away from the wall. Store light china and glass in upper cabinets.

Standard base and floor cabinets can be placed so they cover most of a wall, but gaps may occur where the wall is longer than the sum of the cabinets. Instead of leaving a single large gap at

Incorporate a balanced mix of built-in and freestanding cabinets and appliances, with custom-made details, such as plate racks or open shelving, for the most versatility.

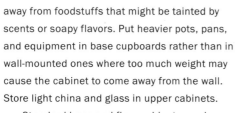

the end of the run of cabinets, you might like to divide the space so it occurs between groups of cabinets. The gaps can then be used to insert a towel rod (if it is a small gap) or a wine rack (if larger), and a space between two wall-mounted cabinets over the sink area is ideal for putting a plate rack. These "leftover" spaces need not be wasted—in some cases, it is better to allow space for a few breaks in a block of cabinets, especially in a large kitchen, to give breathing space to a continuous wall of single-colored cabinets. Plate and wine racks can be bought ready-made, but again you may have trouble finding the right size to

accommodate the space you have—it is like trying to find a missing piece of a jigsaw. To overcome this problem, you could employ a carpenter to custom-build these accessories. If you are working to a tight budget, you can buy the bulk of the kitchen cabinets from a mass-produced range but use the professional skills of a carpenter to add the finishing touches that will make the kitchen unique.

The same applies to the decoration of the doors: you may choose carcasses from a standard selection, but have the doors custom-made, or even buy plain wooden doors and have them painted or decorated to your personal taste, whether it be a simple color wash or a more elaborate effect of cutouts backed with wire mesh or sandblasted glass.

The positioning of cabinet doors themselves is also important. Instead of having all the doors opening in the same direction, usually from right to left, think about the option of having a left- and right-opening door beside each other so you can have easy access to both cupboards at the same time—especially if you store long or large items there, such as a wok or a paella pan. If both doors open to the left, the second door will impede entry to the first cupboard. Corners are particularly difficult areas to equip successfully. Shelves may be

deep and difficult to reach into. In these spaces revolving metal or plastic shelves on a central pivot can make access easier. Also a set of open shelves for attractive large items, such as colored enamel casseroles or stainless-steel pots and pans, can make practical use of an otherwise "dead" area, and as these items are large they will not be pushed to the back of the shelf.

If the floor is uneven, or the wall to which the unit is being attached is not level, the adjustable legs on the cabinets will allow you to make a certain amount of readjustment. Having level base cabinets is not only important for the look of the kitchen—it will be essential when the counter is installed. The surface must be level so things will not roll off; any unevenness also may cause a continuous length of a melamine-topped board or wood veneer counter to bend and eventually break.

Counters should be carefully installed and once in place well sealed. The end edges of work surfaces should be capped off with a matching piece of laminate or, in the case of marble or granite, polished to a smooth finish. In kitchens

Above, left to right **Make sure the type of storage you choose is sturdy enough to cope with the weight of the items to be stacked in or on it.** Opposite **The structural supports of the building are used as part of the storage and decoration of this room. Interesting features, such as these beams, can be incorporated into a scheme.**

where the counter may jut out into a thoroughfare, it may be worth having the ends cut at an angle so they taper to the wall and do not cause bruises to those who may bump into them when passing. Similar care should be taken when hanging overhead cupboards above an area where chores may be carried out, and on the corners of exhaust fans over burners. If the fan casing is being constructed on site, these details can be attended to during the assembly, but if the casing is premade, the corners may have to be capped off with a plastic cover or sanded and rounded when it is delivered.

Plumbing and wiring

During installation, take time to gauge the sites of electrical outlets before wall tiles or backsplashes are in place. Electrical equipment should be used far from the naked flames or heat of a stove and the sockets should be situated away from running water. These aspects should be discussed with the professional electrician who advises you on the wiring and installation of equipment in the kitchen. Sockets should also be placed near cabinets where small appliances are stored and over work surfaces where they will be used so that heavier items such as breadmakers and food processors do not have to be lifted and carried long distances. Ideally the socket should be placed at a height that allows the gadget to be readily used without lengths of cord cluttering the counter. If you place the sockets correctly, it may even be possible to reduce the length of cord on the machine, making it neater and more practical to use.

There are a variety of safety regulations that should be adhered to when your electrical fittings are installed. In the United States, a Certificate of Occupancy, known as a C.O., will not be issued on a new development or refurbishment unless the installations meet the code. Check with your municipal department if you are in doubt about local requirements. Your local housing and planning department may send an inspector to approve safety features before a building is given a certificate. To meet these standards, and for your own safety, it is best to employ a professional electrician to install and wire sockets as well as larger machines, circuit breakers, and high-voltage power cables. Many professional bodies of craftsmen, such as builders and plumbers, issue their

certified members an insignia or seal so reputable tradespeople can be distinguished from "cowboys." These bodies may offer guarantees of craftsmanship and, in some cases, compensation, so when you employ someone ask if they are affiliated to any recognized trade organization.

Most of the new equipment that you buy will come with guarantees and warranties, but if you are renovating an existing kitchen or choose to buy secondhand equipment, this paperwork may not be available. If the appliance is comparatively new, it may be worth contacting the maker direct or asking a local supplier if there is a maintenance service available so that the machine can be checked over and given safety approval, if not a guarantee. If this is not possible, check with a reliable professional; he or she may charge a fee to overhaul the

machine, but this will give you peace of mind that it is safe and worth the money and effort of installing and using it in a redesigned kitchen.

Safety

The kitchen is a hazardous place, with boiling water, pans of hot fat, toxic liquids, sharp knives, and numerous opportunities for accidents to happen. During installation make sure than any risky or potentially unsafe area is made secure and place safety equipment such as a fire exinguisher, in an area where it is quickly and easily accessible, near where it may be needed.

If children have access to the kitchen install door fastening devices to prevent them from coming into contact with poisonous substances such as detergents or bleach. Put guard rails around

Opposite **The low kitchen wall provides a good backsplash area to the sink but allows people in the kitchen to be involved in what is going on in the dining area above. This low wall also makes it easy to pass things through directly from one room to another.**

Above **The same glass-front cabinets are used in both the kitchen and in the dining area.**

Left **Only glass and small items are displayed on the shelving in front of the windows, so light has access to the room.**

Opposite **A ceramic sink is supported by a set of shelves. Pans are easily replaced after washing.** Below **Surfaces in a kitchen should be hygienic and easy to clean. Wood surfaces can be painted or sealed to make them resistant to water or, like this old table (left), covered in a thin sheet of steel.** Bottom **Overhead hanging storage is best kept to the middle of a work area so that you do not bang your head on the suspended pots and pans.**

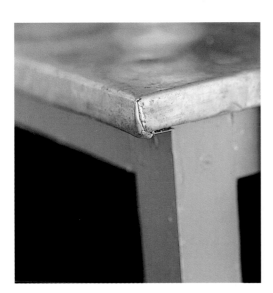

stoves to prevent youngsters from pulling pots and pans down on themselves, and, if possible, install a safety gate across the entrance to the kitchen so younger children do not get underfoot.

Do not keep sharp knives in a utensil drawer where you may cut yourself in the process of searching for them; have a specific wooden or plastic block placed in clear view on the work surface or a wall-mounted magnetic bar so the knives can be kept together in an easily accessible place.

Within the kitchen there should be facilities to deal with an accident should one happen. For cuts and scalds a standard emergency medical kit, available from any drugstore, should be on hand. For fires a fire blanket is useful, as is a hand-held extinguisher. Be sure that the extinguisher you buy is appropriate for its intended use, as some are formulated to deal with electrical fires and others with chemical combustion. If a localized fire does occur, leave the pan or electrical item where it is; do not attempt to remove it until the fire has been put out and the item has had plenty of time to cool down. If the fire is electrical in origin turn the power off at the fuse box before unplugging it. Do not pour water on a burning pan of oil or fat as it may splash and cause burns. Note where the electrical circuit cut-off point is, and the main faucet, which you may need to turn off if the connection to a washing machine or faucet disengages.

During installation make sure you test machines as they are put in. If a stove has serious problems, it will be very difficult to remove once it has been secured in place and perhaps tiled around. Check the position and effectiveness of items such as exhaust fans or vents—if they are too close to the burners the filters may be come clogged with grease and in turn become a flammable source.

Once the installation is complete, take time before you sign any completion forms. Allow a few weeks to try, test, and enjoy your new kitchen and equipment, and if during this "honeymoon" period you find that something is chipped, scratched, or damaged, call the company immediately. Although most firms have guarantees, it may be harder to get them to come back and fix a problem when they have moved on to their next job or when months have elapsed, so make a close inspection as soon as you reasonably can.

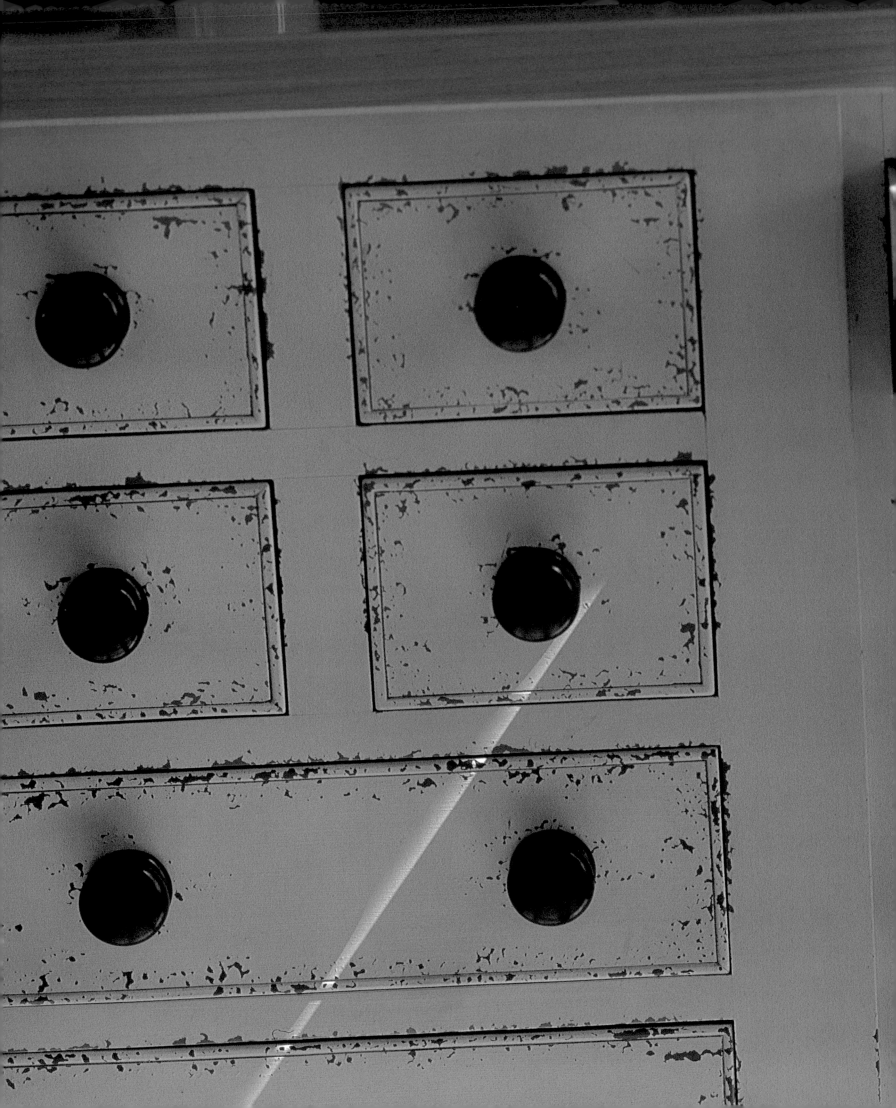

styles

traditional simple country

simple modern new professional

introduction

Choosing the overall style of your kitchen requires just as much thought and careful planning as the selection and siting of the major pieces of equipment. The appearance and design of the kitchen should be one you are going to be comfortable with on a day-to-day basis. There is no point in having decorations and furnishings in a style that will eventually prove to be boring or difficult to live with.

If you are basically a neat person then a full-blown rustic kitchen with open shelves, hanging plates, and bunches of dried herbs may appeal in theory, but irritate you when it actually comes to working there. Conversely, if you enjoy a relaxed approach to cooking and entertaining, you may eventually find the stark lines of a professional-style kitchen daunting. Also beware of the fashionable fads portrayed in magazines. Just because a particular look may be in vogue does not mean it is practical for your home and lifestyle. Look at the reality of your situation—the photographs may show the Manhattan loft of a professional couple who only make coffee. If you live in a split-level house and have a young family, will the open shelves and etched glass of the kitchen in the magazine be durable enough? Are the white walls going to become marked quickly? Be practical and truthful with yourself at this stage to prevent problems later.

In addition to your approach to cooking, take into consideration the setting of the kitchen. Look at the period and style of the whole room. If there are major structural features, such as arches or unusually shaped windows or doorways, they might suggest a certain period or a style that is sympathetic to the surroundings. Equipment is also a factor. If you like retro-style machines, such as 1950s fridges, these may suggest a certain look. But if the style of your existing machines and the decor you want do not correspond, the problem can be overcome; many large appliances can be camouflaged with a fascia to complement the rest of the cabinets.

To help you decide on a style, consider collecting picture references and style pointers. Tear out photographs from magazines and illustrations from catalogs and brochures, and gather swatches of colors, fabrics, or surface materials that you like and stick them into a notebook. Jot down, in a few words or with a sketch, what you like and dislike about friends' kitchens. In a short while you will have built up a visual reference as well as a practical list of dos and don'ts, all of which will help you when deciding on the style of your kitchen.

Opposite **While there are rules to planning and fitting a kitchen, the style of the fixtures and accessories is ultimately a personal choice.**

traditional —a reassuringly cozy and homey environment

The Traditional-style kitchen is perennial; for some people this look never goes out of fashion. The principles of its design are handed down from generation to generation and are based on practical experience, over years of continuous adaptation and use. The basis of this style is essentially historic: it looks back to rural homes where the kitchen was not only the place where food was prepared and eaten, but it was also the main room where the family congregated, talked, drank, and relaxed. This type of kitchen is based on the room that is truly the heart of the home.

There is inevitably a certain amount of nostalgia connected with the Traditional kitchen—it is a reminder of times before high-speed modern life took over; it offers a reassuringly cozy and homey environment that can be understood and recognized by most people. But although the origins of the style may be basically quaint and old-fashioned the look can be modified—it is a matter of personal taste as to which Traditional style you follow and to what extent you adopt the look in terms of decoration.

Certain elements are important to achieve this look. Traditional kitchens can draw inspiration from local sources, but they may also emulate decorative ideas found in other countries—places where the climate and way of life may seem attractive and appealing. For example, homes in cities as diverse as New Orleans or Chicago may use decorative objects, tiles, and colors that are from the countryside of Tuscany, Provence, or Mexico.

Opposite **No other material suggests a Traditional look as much as wood.** Far right **Freestanding cabinets are most authentic for a Traditional-style kitchen, but a mix of freestanding and built-in furniture can be used.** Right **Oil or natural gas ranges are often seen in this type of kitchen.** Below, left to right **The exhaust fan hood has been disguised in a period-style chimney canopy. Accessories are important; this old flatware tray gives the right feel. Small round knobs are appropriately simple. New furniture can be painted and sanded to give an aged appearance.**

Right With its high ceilings, this room is spacious enough to house a large arrangement of cabinets along the end wall, designed to resemble an old-fashioned hutch. The hutch effect is achieved by placing a plate rack over the sink so that dishes, stacked after washing, provide a colorful and interesting focal point. Painting the top and bottom cabinets in different colors gives the room an informal appearance and a less built-in look. The paneled doors, small wooden knobs, and pediment finish on the top of the upper cupboards and large cupboard to the right enhance the Traditional image. To create a practical working area in this space, an island cabinet is placed between the sink and stove areas, creating a basic work triangle. The dining table is placed to one side, clear of the working areas.

Above Old-fashioned brackets are used to support the plate rack and small metal hooks are ready to receive a row of cups or mugs. These sorts of small details are all important in achieving a well-finished, Traditional-style kitchen.
Right In this type of setting a wooden draining board is appropriate—it complements wood used elsewhere in the furniture and has a classic, timeless appeal. It is specially treated to make it waterproof.
Below By simply rubbing or sanding the corners of drawers you can achieve a well-worn look.

Opposite **This stove is neatly built into a disused fireplace, allowing the chimney to be used as a conduit for the flue. The naturally irregular outline of the recess makes it an interesting feature, and two small shelves provide dry, warm storage for drying fresh herbs and spices.**
Far left **Enamel-front stoves are available in many colors, but choose a shade that will last through several changes in decoration: this type of stove is an investment as well as heavy and difficult to install.**
Left **This cabinet has classic handles and a plain steel façade, which blend in with the eclectic mix of furniture.**
Below **Tailor-made to fit the space, this small end-of-counter area is useful for resting dishes and utensils used during cooking.**

Whatever your reasons for choosing a Traditional style of decor for your kitchen, your next step is to decide whether your theme is to be the full-blown old-fashioned look; a modern interpretation that dilutes the antiquarian feel with a careful selection of contemporary introductions; or somewhere in between these two. Do you want a cacophony of color with all the trimmings and accessories or just a subtle allusion to rural roots with a few well-chosen decorative pieces?

The original Traditional look has been updated by succeeding generations: the style has had to adapt to suit homes of vastly different architectural design and to work around contemporary kitchen appliances that even those pursuing the most purist re-creation of a period look would not do without. The open fire and blackened cast-iron range have been replaced with electric or gas stoves. Cold stores, larders, and meat safes have given way to refrigerators and freezers, and the bowl of drawn well water to a sink and faucets, and even that most twentieth-century of inventions, the dishwasher. Although the overall look is reassuringly old-fashioned, the technology, efficiency, and hygiene standards are all up to date; traditional styling conceals the very best of contemporary labor-saving engineering.

For example, a kettle with an antiquated appearance but of current manufacture will be in keeping with the decor of the kitchen but offer modern competence. A row of stylish copper pans may be lined with the latest nonstick coating so that the outward show is conventional but in use they are efficient and effortless. Manufacturers cater to this taste, reviving the coloring, shapes, and even packaging of designs from an earlier period. The New Maid whistling kettle is a prime example of this trend—a design from the 1950s with a Bakelite handle and spout and a rounded metalized body, it is once again a fashionable kitchen accessory. The Beam Balance scales, developed by F.J. Thornton in the 1900s are often

finishes, and counters of wood or tiles. The backsplash could also be ceramic tile or bare sealed plaster. A built-in Traditional kitchen can benefit from breaks and pauses in runs of cabinets, which will create the effect of the kitchen being made from a number of smaller cabinets rather than one continuous line of cupboards fitted on all the walls. If possible try to vary the size of the cabinets—put a double between two single cabinets, then a double next to two singles—so there is variation in the make up rather than clumps of same-size cabinets above and below the work surface.

Some cabinets can be left without solid doors. This device creates open shelving that is reminiscent of an old-fashioned hutch—the type of space where cookbooks, letters, postcards, utensils, and collections of old tins and boxes could be displayed. These showcase areas may have glass-front doors to keep

You do not have to sacrifice labor-saving appliances if you opt for a Traditional-style kitchen—with clever planning they can be integrated without compromising the look.

seen in today's kitchenware suppliers and hardware departments. These typical Victorian scales with a cast-iron and brass base and a removable brass dish and cast-iron weights are found in many kitchens, sometimes as a period-piece decoration, but often as a fully functioning piece of equipment.

Traditional-style kitchens can be built-in or freestanding. A built-in kitchen would offer a more contemporary interpretation of the look, with doors in solid wood, veneer, or painted wood-effect

the items behind them clean and grease free. Plate racks can be installed to hold everyday dishes close at hand or a decorative display of a more prized collection of china.

The freestanding kitchen is more true to the original Traditional kitchen, which would have been an ad hoc collection of hutches, tables, cupboards, and homemade shelves put together to create viable working and storage space. The most vital piece of furniture in the room would have been a

Top left **Indispensable but unattractive modern appliances, such as dishwashers, can be concealed behind panels to match the other cabinets.**
Top center **Plain doors and classic handles lend stainless steel a timeless feel—simple styling can be "dressed" or accessorized to suit most styles.**
Top right **A row of glazed tiles around the sink protects the wooden counter from the worst of water splashes.**
Above **A plain white ceramic sink is the best choice for a Traditional kitchen.**
Opposite **The elements that give this kitchen a Traditional or period feel are the extended plate rack and the brick-shaped ceramic tiles.**

large wooden table on which food was prepared and eaten. The table was the main work surface and the focal point of the room. If you do not have the space to devote to a huge table, the same effect can be created with an island in the center of the room: it will offer the same combined working and dining space but also provide extra storage space in the cupboards below.

Large pieces of equipment, such as freezers, can, if you want, be concealed behind doors or panels so they blend in with the overall old-fashioned feel of the room, but items such as the stove and sink, which will be permanently on show, should be chosen to be in keeping with

the look of the room. A white ceramic sink is suitable for most kitchens in this genre, but if you opt for a stainless steel version it might be worth considering having it recessed beneath a wooden or polished stone work surface so it is less conspicuous.

Colors and materials

Natural materials—historically the materials that were cheaply and readily available, such as wood, slate, stone, terra-cotta, rush, and straw—are all appropriate and can all be used to create a contemporary look as an alternative to the more conventional aged appearance. Wood is ubiquitous: it is used for tables, chairs, cabinets, counters, on floors, and even as paneling on walls. Either varnished to reveal its inherent beauty and to protect its hardworking qualities or painted in a variety of colors, wood is a vital ingredient in creating the Traditional look.

Far left **Tongue-and-groove paneling gives this room a timeless feel that is emphasized by freestanding furniture and open shelves.**
Left **A hutch has been made by placing an ornate cabinet under a row of shelves.**
Below, left to right **The classic curves of an Arne Jacobsen chair contrast with the parallel lines of the wall paneling. The recessed steel sink is modern but its simple shape sits happily in the mix-and-match style of the room. Wooden chopping boards create a pleasing arrangement.**

Accessories are an important part of the final dressing. This is not a clear-surface kitchen, but one where the cook's tools are a feature of the display. Storage jars and utensils, dishes and glassware, bottles of oil and bunches of lavender, garlic, chiles, or herbs are used as decoration: visual stimuli to remind you of the purpose of the kitchen—a place to have fun, to cook, to dabble in the alchemy of mixing spices and flavors.

If the kitchen is also to be the place where you sit and relax or chat with friends, then comfort should be the key word when choosing furnishings. Easy chairs or armchairs, whether the fully upholstered version or a ladder-back chair with woven rush seat and arms, can be used. Harder wooden chairs should be softened with small decorative cushions that can be kept in place with ties or ribbons sewn to the corner and tied to the back legs or back uprights of the chair.

Floors can be wood, brick, terra-cotta tile, or stone, scrubbed and waxed, or sealed. To soften large expanses of floor, mats are often used. Woven straw or reed mats or cotton rag rugs are most authentic, but plain runners or India-cotton rugs can be effective.

If the setting is genuinely old, there may be wooden beams in the ceiling, but if they do not exist you may want to add fake ones. If you do, make sure the wood you use is not too perfect— original beams are old, often gnarled, and irregular although straight. Original beams would most likely have been hewn from a tree trunk by hand, using an adz or hand chisel, the indentations and imperfections adding to the character. Also beware of staining the wood too dark: painting beams black can make them look Tudor rather than Traditional, and they may appear as dominant black lines on a ceiling rather than an integral feature of the room.

Right, clockwise from top left **Glass-front cabinets provide light relief among rows of solid doors. An old beam acts as a backplate for utensil pegs. Sharp knives should be carefully stored; this recess keeps blades out of harm's way. Dried beans and lengths of split bamboo have been used to fill the space behind the glazed panels of these drawers, creating highly original decorative drawer fronts. Pegs or hooks provide hanging space for utensils and tea towels.**
Opposite **Heavy old beams, such a feature of this room, lend themselves to Traditional style.**

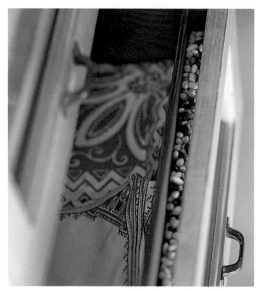

simple country
—a classic
look updated

Simple Country is less cluttered than Traditional style and, although similarly based on old designs, it is has a more streamlined appearance and therefore a greater contemporary appeal. It is a style inspired by American, Northern European, and Scandinavian sources. The look is fresh, neat, and uncluttered, and as in the Traditional style, cabinets are made predominately of wood, sometimes pale and plain but most often painted. In many ways it is a classic look, but it can be updated to make it more fashionable.

For example, the strength of colors used and the styles of accessories such as doorknobs and catches that adorn the basic kitchen may change from time to time. The design of the cabinets and furniture, however, is very much based on specific historic influences or an interpretation of a particular period or geographical region.

One of the strongest contenders of influence is Scandinavian style. This is essentially simple and uncluttered, with liberal use of painted wood. Simple cabinets, plate racks, and hutches are all an integral part, although as with all historically based kitchens, the cabinets would originally have been freestanding, not built in. For inspiration and decorative details look at the paintings of Carl Larsson, whose home at Sundorn in Sweden is where this light and airy 19th-century style is said to have

Opposite **The marble-topped table is reminiscent of French patisseries—it is also the ideal cool surface on which to roll out piecrust.**
Above **Glass shelves provide light and visually pleasing storage space.**
Right **Glass-front cupboards create an open and fresh feeling whereas solid doors might have created a darker and heavier feel.**
Top right **Stationary vertical dividers in extra-deep drawers create well-organized storage space for baking trays next to the stove.**

Left, top to bottom **This classic stove suits all settings. Carved posts on free-standing shelves make an interesting feature. An ornate wirework basket doubles as a glasses carrier.** Opposite **A French café sign and decorative floor tile panels bring color and style to this room.**

been created. Other references may be found in Gustavian style, the more elaborate and ornate decoration favored in the 18th century during the reign of Sweden's King Gustav .

Cabinets in the Scandinavian kitchen may be edged, top and bottom, with simple carved pediments and pedestal details, making the cabinets appear more like finished pieces of furniture than storage cabinets. Where shelves are left open for a display of china or bottles and jars of home preserves, they would be painted and edged with a length of scalloped-shaped cut paper or fine linen—but not too lacy or ornate. Cabinet doors and dado or ceiling borders of simple, stenciled designs are also appropriate, in shades stronger than the cabinets are, but still subtle and muted.

Not all cabinet doors need be solid: panels of chicken wire or finely pleated fabric can be used. If the kitchen has a mix of freestanding and built-in cabinets, a cupboard, similar in size and proportion to an armoire, is a good Scandinavian feature. Again, the cupboard can be made to look lighter and less dominant by replacing the center of the door panels with chicken wire or by stenciling a motif or monogram on it.

Cabinet doors with plain faux panels of painted lines will also enhance the overall appearance and style of the room. To create the effect, choose deeper shades of the base color of the door—for example, if the doors are painted a blue-toned

off-white, faux panels can be created using a band of dark gray with an outer line of medium blue.

Small wall cabinets and painted shelves with decorated plinths are used not just for storage but also to decorate expanses of pale painted wall. These little chests and cupboards can have punched or cut-wood patterns in them or be simply paneled with a few lengths of wooden beading.

Another popular influence in Simple Country design is Shaker, inspired by the religious community that, in the early 1800s, settled in the northern United States, around Maine. Two hundred years later, the legacy of Shaker design, with its clean, uncluttered lines, and the Shaker practice of simple living, is still admired. Although their original furniture designs have been adapted to suit modern materials, homes, and lifestyles, the look has not changed much. To emulate the look successfully it is useful to know a little about the people who created it and why they did so.

The principles of simplicity of design, crafts-manship, and practicality were among the edicts of the Shaker movement, founded by Anne Lee, who originally came from Liverpool, England. In the communities there were many fine craftsmen and women who produced uncomplicated yet beautiful and functional furniture, boxes, and baskets.

The Shaker motto was "Hands to work and hearts to God" and they believed that the quality of their work, even in unseen places such as the back of a cupboard or the inside of a drawer, should always be of the highest standard because God is omnipresent and could see all. Quality is important in simple designs and furniture because there are no frills or fancy dressing to disguise inferior work-manship or clumsy finishes.

The Shakers also recycled furniture: if a bed was no longer needed, it would be disassembled and the wood used to build something else that was required. The uncomplicated nature and qual-ity of their work has made their furniture and style

Top left **A ceramic sink and a wooden draining board highlight the rustic feel.**
Far left **A kitchen table can be as basic as you like. This one is made from a box base with wide planks of mature wood laid across the top.**
Left **For protection from everyday wear and tear wood should be waxed or oiled.**
Opposite **Wood, wicker, and earthenware pottery are important ingredients of this style.**

Opposite **Old china and creamware are at home in the unfussy Simple Country kitchen.**
Far left **Instead of a row of solid overhead cupboards a single glass-front display cabinet and a plate rack are more in keeping.**
Left **Mason jars are useful airtight storage for dried beans and legumes.**
Below left **Neatly arranged on shelves, even everyday plates and foodstuffs can be attractive.**
Below **A freestanding cabinet creates a focal point at the end of the room.**
Bottom **Old storage containers like this flour bin give an authentic touch.**

timeless and original. Antique Shaker furniture is now sought after and collected for contemporary as well as period homes.

Although some people may be fortunate to have antique or authentic furniture, modern copies and reproductions are generally of good quality, and the Shaker style can be successfully re-created by a skilled carpenter or craftsman. Historically the kitchen would not have been built in, but made of large cupboards and chests, with a large scrubbed table, but ordinary built-in cabinets grouped simply around the walls can give a modern version of the original style.

The basic kitchen should have simple, unfussy cabinets, with a plain or tongue-and-groove center panel and a broad relief border. To achieve a kitchen that emulates the authentic look, all white appliances, such as refrigerators and freezers, should be concealed behind doors or panels. It is not that the Shakers were against machines—in fact they were all for labor-saving devices—but the appearance of shiny contemporary pieces of equipment somehow detracts from the purity of the style. Doorknobs should be plain and unfussy—round, polished or painted wood or white ceramic.

The peg rail, another Shaker trademark, is a band of wood with rounded wooden pegs inserted at regular intervals. The rail is a practical storage solution that can be used to hang pots and pans, kitchens linens such as aprons or towels, as well as jugs, mugs, strainers, and ladles—in fact, any kitchen gadget that has a handle and is not too heavy or bulky. In a small kitchen the rail may also be used to hang folding chairs, keeping them off

the floor and providing valuable extra space in the center of the room. The rails were also used to hang clothes and furniture so that the floors could be easily and thoroughly swept and mopped.

Colors and materials

The Simple Country kitchen is devoid of the clutter of Traditional style. Herbs are not hung up to dry or on display; they are stored in neat containers on shelves. The mix-and-match collection of china is replaced by plain white plates and bowls or a collection from a matching dinner set in a low-key pattern. Colors tend to come from a limited palette and are chosen to harmonize and coordinate rather than clash. It is altogether a more orderly look than Traditional style.

Top left **Corridors or foyers can be used for overflow storage.**
Top right **A padded bench is comfortable enough for dining or relaxing.**
Above **Shelves across windows will give extra storage but allow light in.**
Opposite **The rafters and beams, and an abundance of foliage, add to the country feeling.**

Shaker kitchens tend to have white or cream walls with cranberry red, gray-blue, or soft green painted cabinets. Where natural wood is used, it is often the warmer tones of cherry wood rather than the yellow tones of pine. As we know, Shakers were great recyclers, so secondhand planks are ideal for flooring, doors, and countertops.

Continuing the theme of purity of design for which the Simple Country kitchen is known, the Shaker-style kitchen should be made of natural materials; shiny polymer finishes and an abundance of stainless steel would be out of place in this look. Although this style of kitchen may appear to made out of tongue-and-groove planking, the appearance can be deceptive. These days cabinet

doors are often made from composition board that is routed and grooved to look like wooden planks. Once the board is painted it is very difficult to tell real wood from the substitute and composite board can be cheaper and more predictable (it is less likely to warp or bend than real wood).

Ceramic tiles are not generally a part of the Shaker kitchen, but where they are used in areas around a kitchen sink or as a backsplash behind a stove, they are best left as simple as possible. No patterns or fancy borders should be used, just plain white or cream squares that will almost disappear into the wall color. Stone materials, such as ornate or colored marble or speckled granite, are other finishes that are not appropriate to Simple Country kitchens.

In Scandinavian kitchens, colors tend to be pale washes of green, gray, or blue. The fabrics and stencils can be brighter, but they should not be too vibrant, although red, in conjuction with white, can be used sparingly. Checked or striped patterns are popular, as are delicate sprig or floral patterns, but do not try to add floribunda rose prints or Oriental bird designs—think about the floral and fauna native to Northern Europe; they will be the types of motifs most appropriate on printed fabrics. Plain materials can be rich in texture: oatmeal and natural linens, burlap, and jute edged with borders of patterned fabric can be successfully used for pillows, slipcovers, shades, and curtains. Embroidery and cutwork are also in keeping.

Tiles are more widely used in the Scandinavian kitchen and can be a mix of plain and decorative. Again, the patterns should be delicate and subtle, with maybe just a simple border and unobtrusive central design. These tiles should be smooth, unlike the rustic handmade ones favored by Traditional style, and they should be thin.

Painted wooden floors are another feature of the Simple Country kitchen. A plain sanded floor can be edged with an uncomplicated border painted with diluted latex paint or watered-down wood stain. The decoration can be kept simple or made more elaborate—to the degree wherein the pattern assumes the colors and quality of a painted rug. Once the floor has been painted, you can either leave it to age and fade underfoot or seal it with a flat varnish that will make it more durable and help preserve the original strength of color.

Another floor treatment that you may want to consider is bleaching wooden floorboards or pickling them to achieve a lighter, weather-beaten look. The pale tones achieved with these methods can look very attractive with the muted colors of the painted furniture and cabinets, and they can provide a good background on which to put brighter floor coverings such as rugs and mats.

Mats are sometimes seen in Shaker kitchens but they tend to be runners—strips of woven fabric—rather than generous rugs. In other Simple Country kitchens, homespun rugs in colors to suit the scheme are both decorative and useful. If the other fabrics in the room are bright, say a rich blue and white check or a mint green and white design, the colors in the mat or rug could be chosen to co-ordinate with or complement them.

The appropriate furniture and accessories are vital to complete the look. Chairs can be all wood or wood with wicker or woven straw seats. White or painted wicker furniture can also be appropriate. The ladder-back Shaker chair is another important feature that should be added to the kitchen if there is room. The chair is plain and unadorned, with a seat made of woven cloth tape that is comfortable to sit on. Unlike the Amish, another religious community, the Shakers were fond of modest decoration, so the seats are often woven with different-colored warp and weft threads, creating a checkerboard pattern. The two tall upright back posts of the chair are finished with finials or pommels; these were not just decorative but were a practical and easy way to lift and move these lightweight chairs.

Accessories such as enamelware, pewter, and simple bowls and plates are often put on display in the Simple Country kitchen rather than hidden away in cupboards. Fine examples of needlework, such as simple samplers, can be framed and hung on the wall and, if a wall clock is to be added, it should be painted and decorated wood as well. Other typical accessories include the distinctive oval Shaker storage boxes. Once used to hold flour, dried beans, and grain, they now hold cookie cutters, rubber bands, recipes, and small utensils. Baskets were another popular storage container—they were originally hand woven from fine shavings of ash wood. Punch-patterned metalware, such as candle sticks and wall sconces, can also be used to decorate.

Both Scandinavian and Shaker styles of Simple Country can be used in old and more modern homes, and the palette can be varied, within reason, to suit other interior schemes, but the essential ingredients are simplicity and a limited use of color as well as abundant wooden materials.

This page, from top **Elements of Simple Country style include old-fashioned storage jars; fresh linen cloths, napkins, and tea towels, and bringing the outside in, whether it is a bunch of wild flowers or a topiary in training.**

Opposite, clockwise from top left **An old-fashioned pot still makes excellent coffee. Bowls and dishes that do not match are fine. Pots and pans can be left on show. As long as it is clean and safe, faded and worn paintwork is acceptable. Open shelves are attractive, but items should be neatly arranged. Hanging racks come in many shapes and sizes. Keeping small items well stored and in order saves time. Authentic country sinks come in wood, copper or ceramic. Rows of gleamingly clean glassware are always a pleasing sight.**

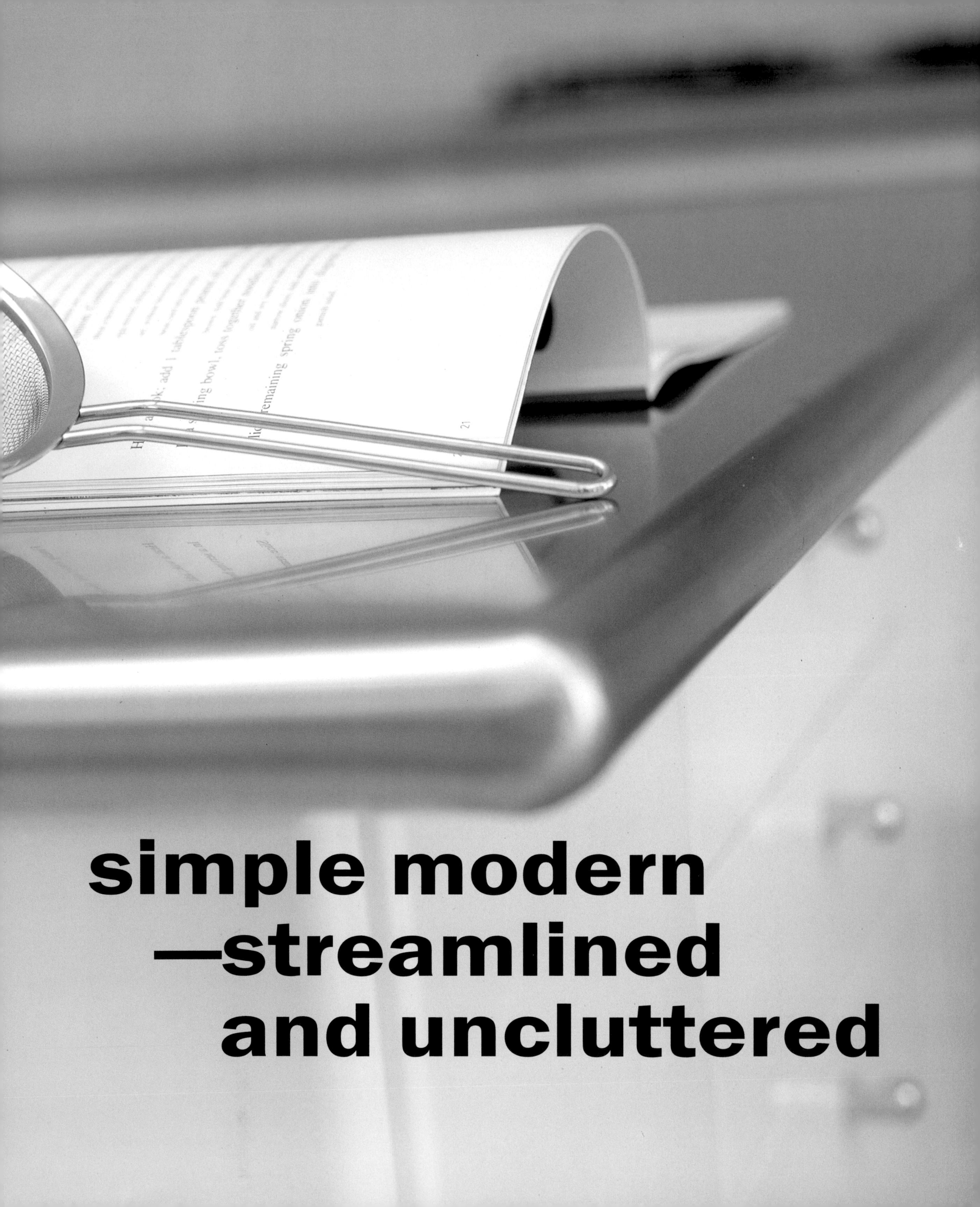

simple modern
—streamlined
and uncluttered

The Simple Modern kitchen is a workplace with a look that is pared down and neat, yet not stark. It is easy to clean and maintain and can be quickly adapted to become part of a family breakfast room or a place for entertaining friends. Although primarily a practical space, there is a certain softness in the fixtures and decor that give it a homey and inviting feel. The overall style is halfway between the high-tech austereness of the professional kitchen and the old-fashioned, conventional country look. Simple Modern is a kitchen design that is increasingly popular, and when you are planning or thinking about this look, bear in mind the old adage "less is more."

With their rationalized shape and uncluttered appearance, Simple Modern kitchens are ideally suited to small apartments and metropolitan dwellings, but they can be adapted and enlarged to suit most settings. In properties where the back of the house has been extended to enlarge the kitchen, especially into a conservatory area or a wall with large sliding glass doors, this look can provide a link between old and new. As it has modern elements and it is not a dramatic statement of a definitive period, it can rest easily in both the original and the new part of the room. With good planning the Simple Modern scheme can be a chameleon, blending and adapting to bridge the two.

Although the basic design principles of being unfussy and streamlined follow the professional kitchen outline, the colors and details come from the mellower spheres of country and Shaker-inspired looks. The simplicity of lines of the Simple Modern kitchen usually extends to having flat door surfaces—no panels, beading, or tongue-and-groove planks—and the cabinet doors may be almost featureless, except for an unembellished handle or rail. This look can be achieved with only built-in cabinets or a mixture of freestanding and built in. For example, base and overhead cabinets could be installed to give a run of

Opposite **The hardness of metal can be softened with rounded corners.**
Top left **Clean, uncluttered lines are essential.**
Top right **This glass-domed kitchen is flooded with daylight.**
Above left **A fine metal rod provides a practical hanging rail.**
Above right **Adjustable slatted shades can regulate the strength of light from the window.**

storage and counter areas, or expanded with the addition of freestanding elements, such as a tall cupboard or sideboard that matches or contrasts with the core kitchen. Although this style is best suited to a linear configuration, it is can be arranged and planned to work in more traditional formats.

The Simple Modern kitchen has to be carefully planned, with work areas and storage and work surfaces designed to cope with the demands of a smooth-running and efficient kitchen. Cabinets are often built to accommodate the many machines and pieces of equipment that are an integral part of today's busy domestic life, such as a refrigerator, freezer, dishwasher, and washing machine, rather than leaving them on show. Larger appliances can be concealed behind panels or doors that match or coordinate with the rest of the cabinets. Disguising or concealing large machines in this way has the effect of playing down the harder, functional, professional side of the room and promoting the softer, more decorative side.

This subtle change of emphasis can also be achieved with the introduction of softer cabinet shapes. Instead of the angular hardness of the professional kitchen, Simple Modern tends to favor round and oval shapes. Cupboards with rounded corners help to create a friendly appearance and are also more suitable for a family to live with, as they are less likely to induce bruises when bumped against. This is not a totally uniform look, so rounded shapes can be mixed with standard square or oblong cabinets. Island cabinets and peninsular bars can also double as breakfast benches or casual dining areas, with the resulting feeling that the kitchen is integrated into the whole living area, rather than being a specific and isolated work place.

Most kitchens in this style will have one of the many home versions of the professional ranges used in restaurants that are now on the market, but some people will opt for the wall-mounted double oven with one, if not both, being a convection oven. Some of the most recent designs of wall-mounted ovens have a flat computerized control panel that is operated by simply pressing the panel with a fingertip (there are no knobs or dials to collect grease or for a passerby to knock against). The door is often clear glass so that cooking in progress can be monitored, but it is so well insulated that little or no heat escapes and the exterior of the door itself remains at room temperature. This type of oven is also available with a choice of a raised bar handle across the full width of the door or a recessed handle mechanisim that pops out when pressed.

Top right **A fake-drawer front panel conceals an ingenious pull-out table.**
Right **A marble inset in the wooden counter next to the stove provides a place to put down hot pots.**
Opposite, clockwise from top left **The hardness of steel is softened with pale lacquered wood and a checkerboard slate floor. A few pieces of well-worn natural materials will alleviate the clinical overtones of high-tech machines and steel. Smart portable shelves hang from a peg rail. Classic, plain white china looks good in any style of kitchen.**

Instead of the large pantry-style combined refrigerator-freezer cabinets, in this type of kitchen it is more usual to have a series of individual refrigerators and freezers built in under the counter. For example, there might be a standard refrigerator for daily use, a small freezer for easily accessible foods, and a bottle refrigerator for wines, water, and soft drinks. This configuration can be advantageous in small rooms or in a space that has a series of angles and corners that make it difficult to allocate the large area of wall and floor space that bigger refrigerator-freezers require.

The few gadgets that are on display in the Simple Modern kitchen should be selected design classics, such as the Phillipe Starck citrus press, the Dualit toaster, or the most modern Alessi kettle or coffee maker. Any old favorites that do not have the requisite sleek appearance can be concealed in a cupboard and brought out only when they are to be used. Accessories too should be specifically chosen to complement the colors and style of the kitchen: even the cookbooks on show should be by celebrity chefs, and recipes on pages torn from magazines are definitely out of place. In its most metropolitan and authentic interpretation, the Simple Modern kitchen is a showcase as well as a serviceable location.

Utensils can be hung from a bar across the back of the counter or on a panel next to the stove. Again, these items must be stylish; if the panel behind them is steel then the utensils should be steel, black, or white. Many modern spoons, can-openers, and vegetable peelers have attractive but very useful thick rubber hand grips. When these

Top left **Steel surfaces are durable but they may scratch; most should be cleaned with a soft cloth and a recommended cream cleanser.**
Top center **Neat metal disks provide useful pot hangers and are positioned so that the top of the hanger protects the wall from the rim of the pot hanging above.**
Top right **The front of this cabinet has been softly curved, giving it a contemporary and less rigid appearance.**
Above **A slim but useful cupboard has been built into a narrow gap.**
Above right **Instead of handles that stand proud these drawers are opened by recessed ovals.**
Right **Mixing unusual colors and flat and shiny surfaces gives a modern feel.**
Opposite **A combination of straight lines and curves gives this kitchen a fresh and interesting appearance. For safety, reinforced glass has been used to glaze the long curved windows.**

items are displayed on a rack, they become a part of the decoration and a point of interest, so it is important that they are the sort of things you will enjoy looking at as well as using.

Lighting this style of kitchen is often done by halogen spot lights—small recessed ceiling lights that are directed to shine on the main work areas. Additional under-cabinet task lighting will also be necessary since this is a serious working kitchen and center lights, if there are any, should be shaded with a classic chrome or a discreet unobtrusive shade, in keeping with the overall no-frills decor.

The Simple Modern kitchen has a broad appeal, with something to offer the single professional, a couple setting up home together, or a growing family. It can be varied in austerity to serve most tastes, from spartan and ascetic to simple and domesticated, without compromising the basic ingredients of the style. This category of design is a good starting point, a useful first kitchen—because the look is simple and understated, it can be added to and adapted as needed. The Simple Modern look is something of a classic and although the machines may become outmoded and the accessories outdated, by changing the handles, faucets, and other details it can be updated with relatively little added expense.

Colors and materials
The decor and style of this kitchen should create the impression that the place is light and airy; if the room itself does not have these qualities, they will have to be created. This can be done by putting skylights into the ceiling, if the kitchen is directly under the roof, or by opening up a side wall to create a big window or french doors. If light cannot be brought into the room by structural alterations then the effect must be artificially created with the use of color and cleverly positioned lighting.

It is appropriate that the colors and materials of the Simple Modern kitchen are from a palette that is bright and light. Colors tend to come from the paler side of the spectrum, a wash or hint of color rather than a rich or jewel shade, though a more random effect of cabinets in mixed paintbox colors can also look good. White is a universally popular color for kitchens, and it is particularly

Opposite **Utilitarian corrugated steel creates an interesting undulating cladding for the backsplash and island cabinet.**
Top left **Carousel pot shelves swing out from a deep cupboard; useful in corner cabinets.**
Top center **Smooth sheet steel has been used to create watertight seams around the sink.**
Above left **Steel also makes a hard-wearing wall covering, resilient to kicks and knocks.**
Above center **A traditional trash can complements the corrugated walls.**
Above **Bright colors zing out against the steel-gray background.**

suited to this look, but it is mixed with other colors and textures to prevent the look from becoming too clinical or bland. Diluted citrus shades such as yellow and green can be used successfully, as can naturally inspired shades such as oatmeal and khaki. These pale colors may be contrasted with a darker version of the same shade.

A very interesting effect can be created using pale-colored cabinets with stainless-steel backsplashes and kickboards. Add a polished gray, black granite, or slate countertop to this muted scheme and the dark band of the counter immediately draws the eye to it and can create the illusion that it floats against the pale background. This can lend a stylishly dramatic touch to an otherwise understated kitchen.

Materials appropriate to a Simple Modern kitchen include the harder surfaces of steel, chrome, granite, marble, and glass, but these can be softened by complementing them with wood. Wood can remain natural or be painted, but the lumbers chosen are usually pale ones, such as beech or maple, or warm shades of cherry or rosewood rather than the darker types, such as mahogany or stained oak, which are best used for period or country styles.

Above **An old cupboard and framed pictures make a homey contrast to the 1950s-style chrome stools.**
Far left **Butchers' hooks from a steel bar provide versatile pan storage.**
Center left **A steel backsplash is heat resistant and easy to wipe clean.**
Left **A ceramic sink with a vented front has a traditional appearance but it blends in with the room.**
Opposite **The striped loose covers on the chairs bring a splash of pattern and color to the kitchen, and provide a change of mood between the working and relaxing areas of the room.**

Glass is widely used in the Simple Modern kitchen. Strengthened glass—plain, opaque, or patterned—can provide light relief from solid composition board or steel-panel doors. Glass doors or inset panels also add a less formal and businesslike finish, as well as make it easier to see what is in the cupboards while keeping grease and dust off the objects inside. Glass is best used in upper wall-mounted cupboards where it is less likely to be smashed, and also where light makes it easier to see into the cupboards, but if a specially toughened safety grade is used to prevent accidents, glass can make an interesting display feature out of a row of floor cabinets.

Manmade materials such as colored laminates and resin finishes are also popular. These new laminates come in a spectrum of bright colors and may have patterns or designs as an integral feature. In combination with plain surfaces they can be used to achieve a lively but not overpowering scheme. They are durable and easy to wipe clean, and require little or no maintenance. Practical considerations such as these are well worth contemplating because this style of room is best kept neat and tidy. Clutter, scuffs, and smears will look out of place and detract from the overall appearance.

Cabinet doors should be a single plain color with practical but stylish handles or bars. The pale background will make the handles stand out as a feature, so it is worth investing a little time and money to locate good-looking, quality door hardware. Handles, railings, and bars work best when they are plain and unadorned in design. Steel is an excellent choice, as is brass, which has a warmer, more mellow appearance.

Left **One-room living—the kitchen, dining, and seating areas are all together. The steel trim in the kitchen is echoed in the chrome frames on the chairs and sofa. The use of the same flooring gives a feeling of unity, but the long row of cabinets forms a definite divide.**
Above left **Storage on display should be neat and uniform.**
Above right **The sink is slightly lower than the counter so that a low backsplash keeps spray in check.**

Top **When choosing handles for drawers and doors try them out to see if they suit your grip and hand size. Also remember that handles may need to be cleaned if grabbed by flour-covered or greasy hands, so avoid anything too fussy or ornate. Where you position the handles is also important. On upper cabinets you should place the handles on a lower edge so that they are within easy reach, and on lower cabinets position them so that you do not bump against them as you are standing at the counter.**

Above **Space within drawers may need to be subdivided to contain smaller items.**

Above right **Long door handles mirror the uprights of the staircase in this modern interior.**

On top of the plain cabinets there should be a long, clean length of counter interrupted only by an inserted appliance such as a stove or sink that cannot be concealed. The wall adjoining the counter is another area where a plain and durable surface should be placed, but it can be in a contrasting material and color to the cabinets and counter. This backsplash area is often punctuated by a narrow utensil rod from which small shelves and kitchen towel holders can be hung.

Ceramic tiles are found in the Simple Modern kitchen, but they are often flat-finished rather than glazed, and for backsplash areas they tend to be

small mosaic-size squares. Shiny surfaces are restricted to the muted sheen of stainless steel and the polish of a chrome rail—highly glazed tiles can look brash and cheap in this minimalist setting. Ceramic colors are usually kept pale and light with little or no decoration, as these tiled areas are not designed to draw attention. They are functional rather than decorative and should blend in with the wall or cabinet color.

By contrasting textures and colors in a scheme you can bring interest and variety without having to resort to overblown patterns. Black-and-white checkerboard tiles may be used in some cases, but apart from a sharply graphic design such as this, Simple Modern is not a look that works well with floral patterns or ornate designs on surfaces or upholstery fabrics.

Floor surfaces can be of wood, linoleum, or tiles, and old floorboards will blend with any color scheme and provide a neutral base for even the more high-tech styles of Simple Modern designs. Again flat finishes are preferable to shiny ones (shiny floor surfaces are to be avoided in kitchens, as they can become dangerously slippery if water or another liquid is spilled on them).

Floor surfaces are best left bare, not dotted with mats or rugs, which belong in other kitchen styles. Even if the room is a kitchen/dining or kitchen/family area, the overall appearance should be unadulterated and fresh. Floor areas can be defined by changing the color and shape of the floor covering itself, to help differentiate between two functions. For example, the floor area of the kitchen could be laid with a pale dove-gray linoleum that curves majestically to the outer edge of the end of the peripheral cabinet. On the far side of this curve, covering the area designated to be the dining room, the tone of the linoleum could change to a deeper charcoal shade.

If you are using wood flooring in a large room that contains two functions, or two smaller rooms have been knocked through to make one, keep the grain and direction of the floorboards in a continuous through line. This will help to give a feeling of length and perspective to the room. If you are laying a new floor, wide planks will achieve a more contemporary look than the traditional narrow boards. There will also be fewer boards needed.

Right When you are deciding which stove to have in a new kitchen remember to think in practical terms, as well as considering how different models would fit in with your chosen style of decoration. Look at the cooking equipment you already have and check whether it will still be suitable for use on a different sort of stove. For example, if you have had a Viking or a traditional range the more robust cookware, pots, and pans that are suitable for that type of use may not be the right thing for modern infrared burners. To get the best results from your burners and stove it is important to have the right equipment to suit the heat source and type of cooking you favor, so be prepared for extra expenditure if you do need to completely replace your *batterie de cuisine*.

new professional
—a practical and utilitarian appearance

Opposite **Practical but not dull, the New Professional kitchen is for the keen cook.**

Top left **For a uniform appearance, machines such as dishwashers should be clad with a fascia that matches the other cabinets.**

Top right **An integral counter and sink has completely smooth lines.**

Above left **Long handles enable drawers to be opened easily from either side.**

Above right **Steel surfaces can be sterilized with boiling water.**

Right **Reinforced safety glass is a welcome addition in contemporary kitchen design.**

The New Professional kitchen gained enormously in popularity in the late 1980s and early 1990s. Today it is one of the most desirable choices of kitchen design, particularly for people planning a new kitchen from scratch (it is not a look that works successfully with a mixture of old and new fixtures, so it is best to start over fresh if you are planning on creating this type of kitchen). Inspired by commercial equipment and locations, the defining feature of this style is its businesslike and functional nature. The sort of cooking, refrigeration, and ventilation cabinets that were originally intended for use in restaurants and hotels came into the home and started the trend for unfussy, clear-cut, serious cooks' kitchens.

The interest in professional catering equipment came about through two channels. First there was an appreciation of the clean, uncluttered lines and large capacity of the apparatus and its easy-to-maintain silvery metal casing. Second came the influence of food fashion, and the trend toward broiled, griddled, and charcoal-seared foods such as vegetables, fish, chicken, and other meats. The conventional ovens that were available for the domestic market could not produce the same effect as the high-temperature eye-level broilers or the charcoal-effect griddles that were available on commercial machines.

Many owners of converted loft and warehouse apartments, where space was not a problem, installed an authentic professional multioven, with extensive broilers and six to eight gas rings, large "walk-in" refrigerators, and steel food preparation areas. The New Professional look is best suited to open-plan living, since commercial-size large-scale equipment requires more floor and height space, and a small galley or cottage kitchen would be overwhelmed by the purists' choice of professional equipment. In time, household manufacturers picked up on this trend and started to produce commercial lines of equipment for the home. These lines were adapted to suit smaller kitchens and lay cooks who were intending to feed a family and friends, not a restaurant full of clients. The new-style stoves were more suited to the home because the high heat output and excessive energy consumption of the commercial ranges were moderated and reduced and extra safety features were incorporated.

Opposite **The high back on this cabinet conceals the work area of the kitchen from the living area.**
Far left **The stove is surrounded by metal casing to match the cabinets.**
Left **Wooden flooring gives a softer, more domestic touch to the professional-style equipment.**
Below left **A wall of sliding glass panels protect the shelves from the grime and grease of the kitchen.**

With these types of ranges, the single basic cabinet stands alone, but it can be added to. For example, a plate warmer can be installed at the side of the stove to keep plates and cooked foods warm and an eye-level broiler can be mounted above the burners or over the built-in charcoal grill. Therefore it is easier to customize this type of range to suit your own individual needs and requirements.

Refrigerator-freezer manufacturers were also quick to respond to the swing of interest toward the larger machines. The ice-making, 100-gallon capacity larder fridge has been very popular in the United States for many years, but in recent years European manufacturers have begun to compete

Inspired by the cult of the celebrity chef and by the large-scale commercial equipment found in restaurant kitchens, the New Professional kitchen has been adapted for the home environment by serious cooks, and there is no compromise on function or form.

with American suppliers. They have increased the size and altered the styling of a number of their machines, and begun importing these into the U.S., enormously increasing the selection available.

When a kitchen is supplied with these larger, more powerful appliances, it is advisable to follow the whole system through and install an effective, full-size, professional exhaust fan to remove cooking smells, grease, heat, and moisture. An open-plan living area will not have the divisions or walls to contain steam and odors so an effective

exhaust fan is particularly important in this style of living space. Also, thinking in terms of size and proportion, if you fit one large unit, such as a stove, the other machines and cabinets should be of a similarly generous scale to maintain the overall balance and appearance of the room .

If you do not have the luxury of a huge open-plan loft in which to install a full-scale New Professional kitchen, but you are nevertheless determined to create the look in your home, you could compromise by selecting appliances that are

designed for the home market but suggest the serious look. Standard 30-inch-wide gas ranges, or dual-fuel ranges with natural gas-powered burners and self-cleaning electric ovens can give the effect and appearance of a commercial range in a scaled-down size. Even some of the more conventional refrigerator-freezers can be ordered with silver or charcoal gray finishes instead of the usual white, or custom-clad in fine steel, all of which give the clean-cut industrial look that is the essence of the professional style.

It may not seem apparent at first from the streamlined effect, but the New Professional kitchen can be freestanding. Although they are heavy, many of the commercial-style ranges can be installed and hooked up to electricity and natural gas, but when it is time to move, the connections can be turned off and (admittedly with the aid of several strong helpers) the range can be moved. A freestanding stainless-steel refrigerator-freezer, with the regulation steel casing, is also a movable feast. Utilitarian metal shelving can be used to provide storage space for dried and canned foods as well as china, flatware, and pots and pans. This can easily be dismantled and reassembled in a different location. Industrial perforated aluminum baskets stacked on a central pivot or arranged on a sliding shelf system, as well as metal mesh hanging racks, can also be taken apart and moved. Sinks and exhaust hoods, with all their main plumbing, ducting, and waste pipe connections, may be a little more difficult to remove, but the majority of the cabinets and appliances of the kitchen are readily disassembled.

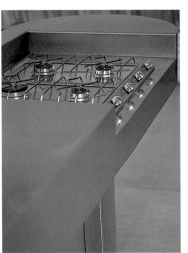

Top left **The support pillar is also a small cupboard.**
Top right **A mirrored wall reflects daylight back into the room.**
Above left **The recessed burners are invisible from elsewhere in the room.**
Above **Long handles are less likely to cause bruises than round knobs.**
Opposite **Two lengths of counter create a galley-style kitchen. Rounded edges soften what might otherwise be an austere layout.**

Sinks are usually molded as an integral part of the work surface on either side. The sink is formed in a long sheet of steel, the sides of which become the work surfaces. This single molded sheet eliminates seams and recesses around the sink where bits of food or dirt might lodge, and because the surface is continuous, it is easier and more efficient to clean. However, it is advisable to use a recommended smooth cleansing cream for these surfaces because many standard products contain tiny particles of abrasive which may scratch and damage the polished steel. Where steel is not used as a work surface, a self-contained laboratory sink may be installed between counters, or a smaller steel sink can be recessed beneath a thick surface of terrazzo, granite, or marble, in a steellike or darker gray coloring. These are all practical, easy to clean, and hardwearing surfaces.

Colors and materials

In minimalist kitchens the choice of materials is crucial, because it is they that create the color, texture, and form rather than peripheral objects such as accessories, pictures, or fabrics. Although the main pieces of equipment, such as the stove, refrigerator-freezer, and dishwasher, might have been adapted and evolved to suit domestic use, the basic professional look and style of the kitchen remains, so it follows that the decoration should, strictly speaking, be clinical, with white walls and tiles and steel counters, sinks, and cabinet doors, but in home settings colors have crept in.

At first the stark white of the true professional kitchen setting was softened with neutral and natural stone and putty colors, then pastel shades were used to soften the hard appearance of the steel cabinets and brushed

aluminum trim. Moving on from these muted shades, some more adventurous designers started to add single, strong colors, such as rich deep blue, acid green, or strong buttermilk yellow, for a wall of tall cabinets, a single area of backsplash, or a length of counter. The use of a single area of vivid color such as this created an attention-grabbing highlight in the otherwise monotone surroundings. Other compromises that have occurred as the look became established include the use of opaque reinforced glass for door panels instead of steel or brushed aluminum, which again serves to lighten the overall appearance. The backsplash area behind the counter and sink, in both the professional and the adapted professional kitchen, are predominately steel, although reinforced opaque glass panels are again used to give a lighter appearance. Sometimes polished black granite or sealed slate is used, but this tends to give a harder and darker appearance to the scheme.

In a professional hotel or restaurant kitchen, the utensils and storage jars would be kept off the work surfaces and stored in pantries and the outer work areas. In practice, these items tend to find

Left **The New Professional kitchen is low key in color and embellishment so any other furniture in the room will stand out against this neutral background. These classic seats by Charles Eames, Alvar Aalto, and Marcel Breuer are perfect in this type of setting.**
Above **A deep steel kickboard brings the metal of the counter and the backsplash to floor level, giving a finished look to the scheme.**

This page, left to right **Thick glass tiles
conceal built-in lighting. The use of
steel extends to the utensils.
Wooden chairs and a round table
soften the hard-edged kitchen.**
Opposite, clockwise fom top left **Steel
surfaces reflect light. A wall-mounted
stove fits perfectly. Marble and stone
are compatible with steel. A gleaming
surface always looks good.**

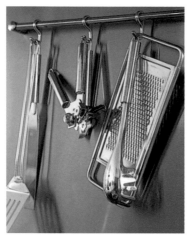

their way back into the domestic kitchen but, in the spirit of the New Professional style, storage jars tend to be matching sets, rather than an eclectic hodgepodge, and utilitarian materials and shapes. Utensils, again mainly made from aluminum, chrome, or steel, in uniform style, are hung from businesslike metal rods or wire racks.

Although the overall features and styling of the New Professional kitchen are futuristic and modern, the flooring is often made from more conventional materials. In lofts, warehouse apartments, or other homes where wood flooring exists it often remains, although it may be sanded to give a clean, fresh

Gleaming uncluttered surfaces reflecting light-filled interiors, sleek architectural lines, and state-of-the-art appliances and gadgets are the hallmarks of a New Professional kitchen.

appearance and sealed with a flat varnish instead of a stained or high-gloss finish. Pale sandstone or slate tiles complement the look well, as does sealed composition board, linoleum, rubber flooring, or epoxy resin-coated concrete.

As light is important in all kitchens, but especially this one, windows should be simply clad with plain shades or shutters that can be folded back into a minimal space when not required. Fabric curtains will only become soggy, steam damaged, and stained, so it is best to leave them for a living area. If the room is overlooked so that privacy becomes an issue, you might

consider putting opaque glass in the lower half of a window, leaving the top in clear glass to allow in maximum light and to create a feeling of space. Artificial lights can be recessed into the ceiling or under wall cabinets and directed so they specifically illuminate counters and cooking areas, but with highly reflective surfaces, such as steel, chrome, and aluminum, in abundance, you have to be careful to angle the lights to avoid glare and flare. Halogen spotlights are the ideal choice.

As this style of kitchen tends to be linear, with the cabinets and appliances along one main wall or divided between opposite or adjoining walls, the straight, parallel lines of the layout are often emphasized by the use of full-length chrome, satin nickel, or polished steel handles on the cabinets. These handles stretch across the width of a cupboard door or cabinet, and are practical because you can grab them and pull the door open at any point along the handle rather than having to grip a specific small knob in the center of the outer edge of the door. Hardware, such as handles, tend to be chosen for their simple style and practical qualities rather than pretty styling.

These qualities also apply to the choice of faucets. In many cases industrial lever faucets are chosen because they are easier to turn on and off with an elbow when your hands are greasy or covered in dough or flour. But for the very reason that they are easy to turn on and off, such faucets can be wasteful of water, so they may not conform to local building regulations. To make certain, check with your area's planning department before you have them installed. Single-spout mixers are always popular because of their minimalist appearance and because they make it easy to supply the right temperature of water from a single nozzle.

Other practical considerations include the location of electrical outlets. These are usually located along the wall nearest the work surface where electrical appliances might be used. In the New Professional kitchen they may be concealed beneath the edge of an island or peninsula work station, or grouped in blocks and covered with a protective shield that can be flipped up to give access to the sockets. Light switches may also be covered in a silvery steellike casing so they are in keeping with the rest of the surface area.

When it comes to adding furniture such as tables and chairs to this style of kitchen, you are in fact deviating from the original plan—in a real

professional kitchen there simply would not be a dining area. The chef may have a small dining table in his office where he can entertain guests, but essentially the professional kitchen is a working area, a place of frenzied activity where there is no time to sit around relaxing and sipping coffee.

If a peninsula or island unit is in the plan, then streamlined stools with silvery chrome or steellike legs would be in keeping, but as with the floors, which may be traditional or old wood, the furniture most often used in this style of kitchen is not necessarily high-tech or avant garde. Arne Jacobsen "Ant" chairs, with their distinctive rounded back and seat, are ubiquitous, even though they were

designed and originally produced in the 1950s. Aluminum "Push Boy" trash cans with flip tops are also retro style, but suitable for this modern look.

When buying china, glass, and flatware for this kitchen, think workmanlike and practical. Plain white china, unfussy flatware, and simple, clear glass are the ideal (in many hotels and restaurants plain white china is used to concentrate attention on the food rather than the fancy rim of the plate). It is also easier to replace a broken white plate than to find the exact match for a colored or patterned version. You can also mix various styles and types of white plates—because they are all the same color, the table setting retains a unity.

Opposite, clockwise from top left
Maximum exposure is part of the New Professional look: working parts such as pipes and ducts may be left on show if they look good. A triangular metal bracket on the counter breaks up the parallel lines. Racks and rails for storage ensure everything is easy to reach.

This page, clockwise from top left **Sleek, featureless cabinets marry well with the regular lines of the rest of the kitchen. A well-planned run of cabinets fills a compact space. Professional-style equipment has been scaled down for domestic use.**

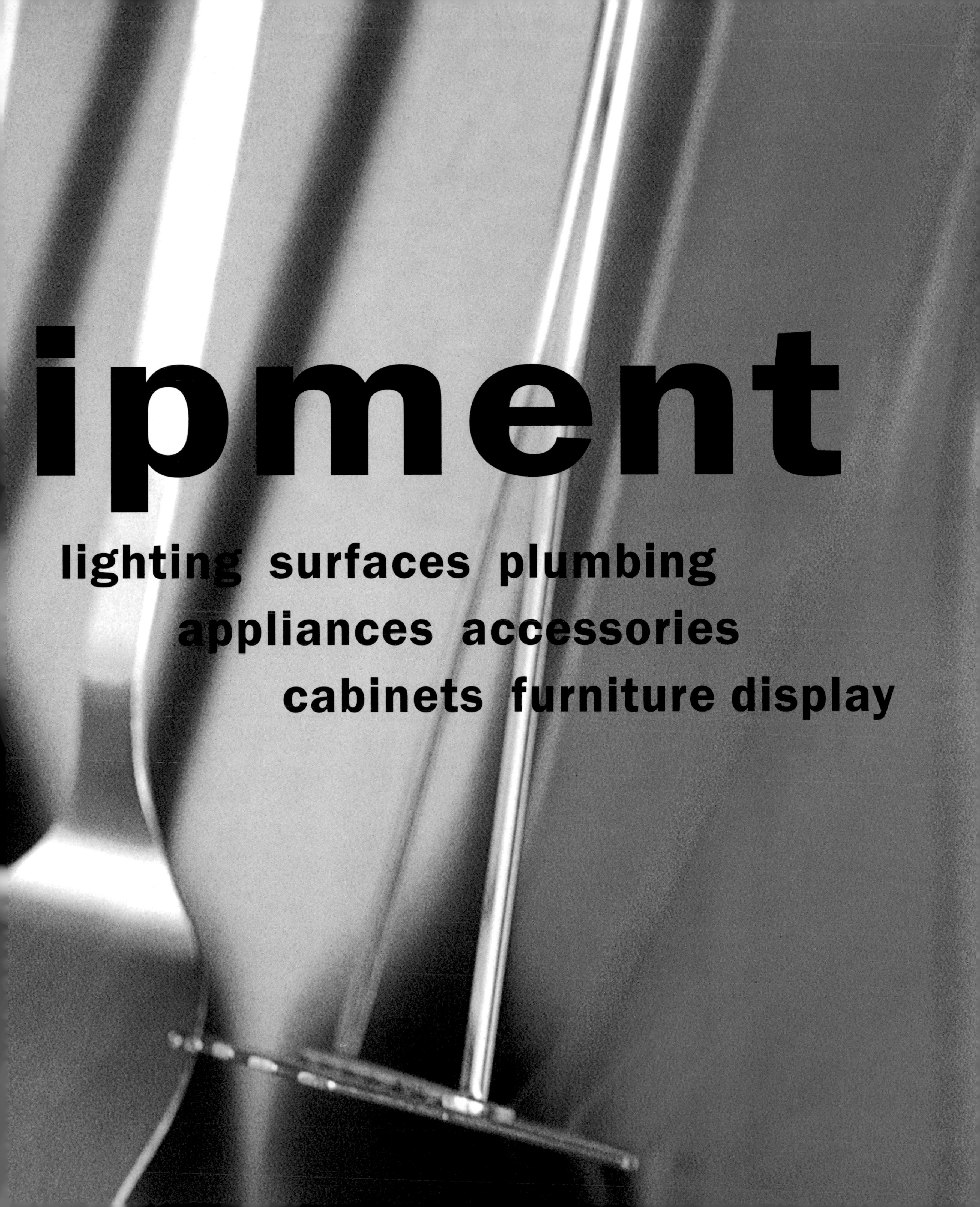

ipment

lighting surfaces plumbing
appliances accessories
cabinets furniture display

introduction

Once you have decided on the structural layout and style of your kitchen it is time to examine the details, such as the finish for doors, floors, work surfaces, and backsplashes, as well as the equipment, both large and small. There is a bewildering assortment of choices in each category, so it is wise to set a price limit and be sure of your requirements before you make a commitment to buy.

Before the cabinets and work surfaces are installed, figure out your lighting plan, so the wiring and fixtures, which may need to be recessed into the ceiling, can be put in place. With wall and counter surfaces, the choice can be narrowed down to those materials that are suitable for the style and color of kitchen you have chosen. Price may play a part in your choice: some finishes are attractive but expensive, and a cheaper alternative might be available that creates a similar look but is still within your budget. You may also be influenced by the amount of time you plan to live in your home.

When you are choosing equipment, spend time visiting showrooms and reading magazines and manufacturers' literature about the latest technology and gadgets. Advances in engineering and energy-saving devices have come a long way in recent years. Whereas you might once have bought a microwave oven that cooked but did not brown, now there are machines that can do both. But even the mighty microwave may disappear in time, as the facilities it provides are incorporated into regular cooking appliances such as a range or stove. Among the latest appliances are those that combine the versatile cooking abilities of natural gas with the microwave's speed, reducing conventional cooking time by as much as 50 percent.

Developments in environmental areas of design and production are having a decisive influence and will continue to do so. There are ecocycles in washing machines and dishwashers that can be used for smaller and lightly stained loads, saving water and electricity. The market for single-household equipment has also grown, with demographic profiles showing that more people live alone. Manufacturers now supply machines to meet these requirements and are becoming increasingly open to tailoring or creating designs to more individual requirements.

So when you embark on the difficult task of buying equipment be sure in your own mind what it is you want the machine to do, but keep an open mind, since you may find that where there used to be a number of separate machines to perform a variety of tasks, there is now one that does them all.

Opposite **Once the skeleton of your kitchen is in place, it is time to fill it with all your favorite gadgets and tools.**

lighting

Lighting is a complex topic but one that is very important in a kitchen. It is best planned in conjunction with a professional, and it should be installed by a qualified electrician. Most people want light, sunny kitchens, but due to location or the direction of the windows it is not always possible. To create the sunny look, as well as a safe and efficient kitchen, artificial lighting should be carefully chosen and well installed.

In addition to achieving the right ambience for the room, lighting is vitally important for safety reasons— to illuminate surfaces where you will be using sharp knives and where there are hot rings or ovens. Storage areas should also be efficiently lit, whether by individual miniature fluorescent strips activated as the door is opened or by spotlights.

Lighting is divided into two main categories: ambient and task. Ambient light is used to illuminate the whole room. Ideally it should be on a dimmer system so it can be adjusted to suit the required mood. The main lighting may be provided by recessed spotlights, supplemented, if necessary, by a pendant or feature light over a table area.

A hanging light has both an aesthetic and a functional role in that it helps to break up the mass of horizontal lines created by rows of cabinets, and may also make a high ceiling appear lower. Some pendant lights come with variable-height

Opposite **Louvered blinds can be adjusted to direct the angle and amount of light.**
Right **Two large inset windows bring daylight to this kitchen, while a candelabra offers a more romantic form of lighting for the evening. Another hanging light provides an electrical alternative, useful on dark winter mornings or dreary afternoons when candlelight would be out of place.**

Above **A central light is a useful addition in a kitchen but will not be sufficient on its own—task lighting will be needed to bring direct light onto working areas.**

Above right **Adjustable lights that can be angled to focus on a particular surface or counter area are very useful. They can be discreet recessed spotlights, miniature strip lights, or more decorative fixtures such as this stainless steel cone.**

Opposite **A dramatic line of silver shaded lights creates a feature in this room, and they cast numerous pools of light beneath them. Wired to a dimmer switch, the light may be altered from bright to soft as needed.**

mechanisms, which mean they can be pulled down low over the table for intimate suppers or raised for other meals and tabletop activities.

Task lighting, which is light targeted at specific work areas, can be created with small fluorescent strips, a low-voltage mini halogen fixture, or strips of tiny bulbs in a rubberized casing, like Christmas tree lights in a transparent garden hose. The latter offer edge-to-edge lighting under a cupboard and a soft but clear overall span rather than a specific or directed spot of light. Task lighting should be positioned at the front edge of upper cabinets rather

than toward the back, because bulbs placed at the back of the cabinet will illuminate the wall rather than the counter area where the activity is taking place. The correct positioning is important; badly positioned lights will cause your hands, and in some cases your body, to cast shadows over the task you are performing, hindering your view and consequently your safety.

Other areas where task lights will be useful include the sink and stove. Lights can be installed under the exhaust hood, if there is one; if not, they could be recessed into the ceiling above or suspended from a gantry and pointed at the stove. The light from these overhead fixtures can be directed more specifically by using a baffle, or shield, so there is a direct beam rather than an amorphous pool of light. At the sink, both the bowl and the draining board should be lit. This may not seem necessary if the sink is in front of bright sunny windows, but at night or on dark winter afternoons, the artificial light will compensate for the lack of natural light, making it easier to see if the dishes are clean and that boiling water or the contents of draining pans hit their target.

If you have high-gloss resin or stainless-steel surfaces, be careful that lights do not cause glare—this can be minimized if the bulbs have a frosted or opaque finish. Other counter and wall materials such as dark shades of granite or slate will absorb

a lot of light, as will a lot of dark wood cabinets, so more lights or bulbs with increased power may be necessary.

Types of light

There are three main types of light available: halogen, which is a very clear white light; incandescent, which is the softer yellow light that most of us know; and the very bright and powerful fluorescent. Ideally, you should use more than one type of bulb to light the kitchen. A mix of halogen and incandescent light can create a good overall effect.

Left and above **This adjustable light can be angled to direct the beam onto the sink, but for an evening meal, the beam can be directed at the wall for a softer diffuse effect.**
Opposite, from top **The choice of bulb is important—watt strength and non-reflective or reflective bases will affect the strength and quality of emission. A row of small lights gives better illumination than a single strong beam that might cause hard shadows. The wide base of this shade allows a broad beam of light to highlight the table.**
Opposite, far right **The openings in these decorative ceramic shades create several smaller pools of light.**

Incandescent lights are fine for general room lighting, but you can do better for task lighting. Halogen bulbs are generally very small and fragile, and should not be touched directly as grease from the skin may damage the bulb—always hold halogen bulbs in a clean cotton cloth when placing them into sockets. The bulbs are tiny, so they are unobtrusive and very suitable for recessed ceiling lights. They last longer than incandescents so they do not need to be replaced as often, a bonus when the light fixture is inaccessible. The light given off by a halogen bulb is clear, bright, and white, but the bulb itself can become very hot, so do not install it at lower levels or in areas where a hand or arm may come in contact with it. If a clear halogen bulb is too bright, try a frosted type that will give a more diffuse and less glaring beam.

Incandescent bulbs give a yellow hue, and the output of light can be varied by using a dimmer switch. This type of lighting is not good for food preparation areas, but it has a softness that makes it ideal for the dining and relaxing areas of the room. Incandescent bulbs have a shorter lifespan than fluorescent or halogen bulbs and can become warm to the touch.

Fluorescent strips were popular in the 1960s and 1970s, but the blue, bright lights have come a long way since then. Fluorescent tubes can now be bought with light and color equivalents to daylight. Fluorescents are also energy efficient, lasting up to

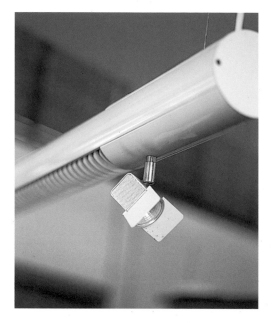

Top left and above **Two in one—this long strip light provides a continuous line of light over the counter, and its tubular shape reflects the steel pillar. It is also functions as an accent light: the attached small spotlight can be directed onto a single object or onto a snack supper on the extended bar area behind the backsplash.**

Far left **Under-cabinet lighting is important not only for safety when preparing food but also to make it easier to find and identify items stored there. A glazed panel built into a narrow gap next to the cabinets throws light into the rest of the room.**

Left **A Hollywood-style arc of light creates a decorative and effective frame for the window.**

Opposite, top **Spotlights in the shelving light the room while recessed lights under the exhaust hood create pools of task lighting over the stove.**

Opposite, right **Narrow strip lights like this can be placed under overhead storage for countertop illumination. Depending on your style of decor, you may want to reveal or conceal them.**

20 times longer than an incandescent bulb, do not cast such strong shadows as other lights, and are cool so they will not add to the heat in a busy kitchen. However, they are powerful and bright and should not be looked at directly.

A standard, integrated lighting scheme for a kitchen involves all three of these bulbs to create various moods and setting. For example, for food preparation, fluorescent strips under cabinets, and halogen spots over the stove, sink, and main island work area can be used in conjunction with halogen ceiling spots and ambient incandescent pendant light. When the food is prepared and cooking slowly in a casserole, the main lights can be turned off and a specific task light left on so the cook can come in and check the food's progress. When dinner is served, the ceiling spots can be turned off, and the wall and ceiling lights, both with incan-

descent bulbs, can be dimmed to provide a soft light to complement the candles on the table.

The kitchen is a greasy and steamy place, so it is worth covering the base of recessed lights with clear glass shields or finding lights that have a cover already incorporated in the design. It will be easier to wipe the glass disk than to try to squeeze your hand into the recessed metal casing around the lamp for cleaning, and the disk may also offer a certain amount of protection for the light fixture.

Switches are best kept simple and easy to wipe. Fancy Victorian-style brass and wooden switches are difficult to operate if hands are sticky or soapy, whereas flat push switches can be activated with an elbow. If the kitchen is large, it may be wise to have switches for the main light on both sides of the room so you do not have to walk from one side to the other in the dark.

surfaces

After the lighting has been installed, it is time to decide the materials you want to use for the major surfaces in the room—the cabinet doors and the counters. These large expanses of color and texture will dictate the character of the room more than any other element in the kitchen.

Opposite **A recess in a polished concrete counter holds a chopping board securely in place.**
Below **Smooth curves give a softer and more modern finish.**
Right **Recessing burners into the surface makes them easier to clean.**
Below right **Concrete, composition board, and maple add variety.**

Counters and backsplashes

The priorities for a countertop are that it should be hygienic and easy to wipe down as well as resilient enough to withstand the temperature of hot pots and pans. It should be wide enough to accommodate counter machines and gadgets and still leave space at the front for food preparation. The material used for the surface should also be sturdy so that the occasional sharp blade or skewer will not inflict lasting damage—although in theory all chopping should be done on a board, some-

times a knife may slip, so the surface should be resistant to sharp points.

Where possible, a countertop should be made from one continuous length of material or, if that is not practical, with as few seams as feasible. Crumbs and debris will accumulate in seams and seals and they can be difficult to remove and clean out thoroughly. The length of a counter will be dictated by the layout and design of the kitchen, but guidelines indicate that an adequate work area should be at least 36 inches long and preferably with easy access to the sink. If more than one person cooks in the kitchen at a time, ideally each cook should have a work surface of this size.

Backsplashes can be constructed from a continuous run of one material or made from a collection of ceramic tiles with grouted edges. This area has, in recent times, become an additional hanging and storage place for spice racks and utensil holders. The backsplash, as the name suggests, is the area where bits of flying cake mix or orange pulp will land when a mixing machine or fruit juicer is in action, so it should be a surface that is water resistant and easy to clean and maintain. The other area to be careful about is the seam between the counter and the backsplash. There are flexible rubber sealants available that can be piped along the seam to create a filling, but a narrow varnished wooden strip or a length of V-shaped plastic joining wedge may be equally effective and possibly more attractive.

Materials that can be used for counters and backsplashs include natural stone such as marble and granite, which generally come with a polished finish, and slate, which needs to be professionally sealed to prevent the stone from flaking. For the backsplash, the stone needs only to be of veneer thickness, as it does not have to withstand pressure or weight, but for the counter it should

be thicker, so it is more robust and solid. The coolness of stone is a boon in food preparation, especially for those who make pastry.

A recent innovation in stone surfaces is Pyrolave, made from volcanic lava stone. Pyrolave is made from a material that has been fired in the earth's own kiln, at temperatures that are hard to comprehend, so it will easily withstand the hottest dishes and pans a home kitchen can come up with. Pyrolave is cut using high-pressure water jets. Surface design and texture can be applied via a computer or the stone can be smoothed and polished to reveal its natural qualities.

Although stone is hardwearing, strong, and will not be adversely affected by heat, the surface may be scratched by a sharp knife or blade. It is also easy to wipe clean, and unless it is sealed with a sensitive finish, it can be wiped down with disinfectant and powerful cleaning agents. The weight is a significant factor. A length of marble counter, for example, can be extremely heavy, so make sure the cabinets or struts underneath them are sturdy enough to give ample support.

Wood is often used for counters or as an inset into an area of countertop, but not often as a backsplash. If you are concerned about reports that wood can be a breeding ground for bacteria, especially salmonella, use a plastic or marble insert or chopping board for food preparation. Some wood is kiln dried and finished with oil or varnish to make it more resilient; other wood is left to dry naturally, and can be waxed or oiled. Although all work surfaces can be made of wood, some people choose to use it in conjunction with materials such as marble or steel, so there are different surfaces for various parts of the food preparation routine.

Maintenance of wooden work surfaces is important; they should be wiped down frequently, (avoid harsh detergents) and be thoroughly dried after use. Although strong and long lasting, wood will be scored and marked by hard knives and burned or scorched by hot pans. In some cases these blemishes can be removed by rubbing with sandpaper and reapplying the top finish.

Ceramic tiles are fine for backsplash areas but really impractical for counters. Ceramic tiles themselves are easy enough to wipe clean, but the numerous grooves and ridges formed by the seams and grouting become full of dirt, and the white grout soon becomes stained with coffee, fruit juice, or just grime. Unless you use a minimal number of very large ceramic tiles or are prepared to bleach or regrout regularly between tiles, it is best to avoid

them on the counter area. They may also chip or crack if a heavy pan is dropped on them.

Laminates are widely available, reasonably priced, and come in a wide selection of colors, patterns, and finishes, from plain white to marble. This surface is stain-, abrasion-, and damp-resistant, but sharp knives and hot pans can cause damage and scorch marks. It sold in generous lengths, so there need only be minimal seams in the finished surface, which makes it good for both counters and backsplashes. Laminate surfaces are low maintenance and long lasting, but avoid textured finishes—the small indentations and undulations, such as those used to achieve a wood-grain effect, can be difficult to clean well.

Stainless steel is an increasingly popular work surface and backsplash material. Countertops

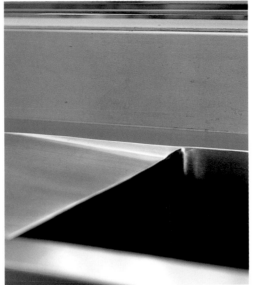

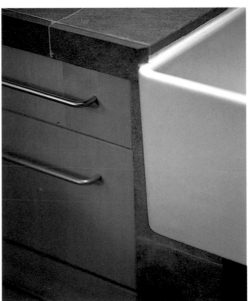

tend to be custom-made, although some manufacturers do have standard-size options. Sheets of steel can be formed to include integral sinks and prestamped drainage boards. These are advantageous because they cut down on the number of seams and joints. Where seams are unavoidable, the two pieces of steel can be welded with an almost invisible seam. This is not only hygienic and practical; it gives an attractive overall appearance.

In general terms, thicker steel is best for countertops; ideally it should be at least ⅟₁₆ inch thick. If the steel is too thin the counter may bend and flex under pressure.

Steel is hardwearing and, if well maintained, it will last a lifetime. Although hot pots will not affect the finish, scratches and dents may show, but lighter marks can be rubbed away with a gentle cream cleanser. Although scratches can be disheartening when the kitchen is new, in time the marks of general wear and tear blend together and

are no longer noticeable—in fact, they can create a less hard, more polished effect. Some suppliers recommend special nonabrasive cream cleansers to be used on steel surfaces since they reduce the incidents of scratching during regular cleaning.

Solid surfaces come in a variety of guises. Polyester, thermoplastic, and acrylic resin finishes have made their way from the chemistry lab to the kitchen and offer a wide choice of durable, easy-to-clean surfaces. Also within this category are the surfaces made with natural materials and resins, reconstituted to form new products.

The new natural and man-made mix surfaces include Erbistone, which has a base of 95 percent quartz that results in a granitelike appearance with durability and hardness similar to the original stone. Corian®, which is constructed from two-thirds natural minerals combined with a high-performance acrylic, can be finished to appear as marble or granite or in a choice of plain

Left top **By using a darker border around the pale interior surface of the cabinet, the overall height is optically reduced.**

Left bottom **Gaps between tiles are traditionally grouted, but in a kitchen it is advisable to make the joints as small as possible since grout can stain.**

Right **Space under the stairs has been made into useful storage. The contrast of colors and surface finishes becomes a feature of the scheme.**

Below left and right **A country-style mosaic effect has been created using marble set into concrete.**

colors. It also has the advantage of being very easy to bond to another piece, making seams and joints almost invisible.

Sheets of these materials can be grooved so that an integral draining board and sink can be created in the counter, a smart way of banishing the difficult seams between the counter and the sink rim. Some of these surfaces are slightly "soft" and have a warmer feel than the real stone surfaces. They can be scratched, but minor abrasions, if not too deep, can be easily sanded away. The main disadvantage of these materials is that they lack the luster of real stone or marble, and it is recommended that they be installed by professionals, which may bump up the overall price.

Cabinet doors

These will, in most kitchens, be the largest and most defining surface areas. The color, style, and type of door you choose will be a major part of the overall design scheme. The doors will need to be hardwearing—capable of withstanding kicks and bangs—as well as easy to clean. Bear in mind that the more ornate features, such as carved panels, beading, and frames, that are added to the door, the more grooves and niches there will be in which grease and grime will collect, which, in turn, will require more cleaning.

Wood is a popular finish for cabinet doors and it comes in three categories—hardwoods, softwoods, and veneers. Hardwoods, such as maple, oak, and cherry, are classic choices, but if the door is made of solid wood, it can be heavy and expensive, though it should last for many years. This type of door is easy to clean with a damp cloth and mild detergent, but will, if sealed with oil or wax, need regular reapplications of the finish. Softwood doors, such as those made from pine, are often stained or painted, as the wood is comparatively

cheap and in its natural state tends to be pale or yellow in color and lacking in interesting texture. If the doors are painted, stained, or varnished, they are easy to clean with a damp cloth.

Veneers are thin layers of wood which are glued to a backing. They have the advantage of being lightweight (if they are applied to a lightweight backing material such as particle-board), and less expensive than solid wood but they can create the same overall effect. With both veneers and solid wood, it is important that the direction and line of the grain match. Another point to remember is that all wood panels, doors, and trims must be given time to acclimatize to the conditions of the kitchen or a room with similar humidity and temperatures so it will not warp or crack when installed.

Laminates can be divided into two categories—high pressure and low pressure. High-pressure laminate is made from compressed resin and paper glued to a backing. Doors made from this material are generally plain, as it is not advisable to carve or rout the surface, but they are easy to clean and hardwearing. Low-pressure laminate, known as melamine, is cheaper, thinner, and less durable than the high-pressure type, but is easy to clean and can be useful for rented apartments or in kitchens where a long-lasting surface is not required. Melamine is also often used to line the carcasses of kitchen cabinets.

Polyester and resin-finished doors are usually in the top end of the price scale. A wide variety of pastel and brilliant colors can be achieved and given a high-gloss, almost lacquerlike, finish. These finishes are durable, but deep scratches and dents are difficult to repair.

If you get bored with your surroundings and like to redecorate regularly, it may be advisable to choose cabinets dressed with a surface that can be painted or altered easily, rather than having to incur the expense of buying new doors each time you fancy a change. Simple plank or framed particleboard or pine doors can be painted several times with no detrimental effect. Laminates or other finishes with a high gloss may be difficult to paint or alter successfully. Painting board or cheaper wood doors will give the whole kitchen a fresh look—a good way of revitalizing a dated or well-worn room.

Opposite The contrast of the roughly hewn wood on the upper cabinets and the smooth surface below gives an interesting emphasis.

Left The wood was left with its natural undulating curves rather than sawn into straight planks.

Below **A small air vent allows air to circulate freely.**

Bottom, from left **Unusual knobs accentuate the rough wood feel. The cupboards appear to be suspended from the beam but are also supported by metal struts. A freestanding cupboard echoes the finish of the wall cabinet.**

Opposite **Fine metal mesh gives the impression of a door but allows light and air to circulate. It is also used to customize the refrigerator for uniformity.** This page, clockwise from top left **Opaque frosted glass makes the door appear lighter but conceals the cluttered contents. Try to maintain a similar feeling between the type of finish used on the cabinets and accessories such as handles or knobs. A contrasting-color knob can become a feature on a door. Unusual shapes and designs of door furniture are eye-catching, but should be reserved for cabinets that do not get too much wear and tear or need frequent cleaning. The center "wedge" of steel gives an otherwise plain kitchen a modern twist. Many metal handles come in matte or polished finishes—the choice is personal. Even old materials such as wicker or cane can be used in contemporary kitchens. Different shapes but the same finish: a mix-and-match effect gives a quirky twist to drawer knobs.**

plumbing

In these days when dishwashers are increasingly popular, a good-sized single sink may fulfill all your water supply and drainage needs, but in a busy household two sinks may be needed to cope with overflow dishes and food preparation. It may also suit your work style to have two sinks, but in different areas. For example, in a large kitchen it could be useful to have a food preparation sink near the refrigerator and vegetable rack and another near the dishwasher and china cupboards for handwashing and storing fine glass, china, or flatware.

Sinks

There are various shapes of sink to consider, from the single, which, if it has a generous-size bowl may be large enough if used in conjunction with a dishwasher, to the multisink. The double sink is still very popular, with one bowl used for washing and the other for rinsing. The triple sink usually incorporates a waste disposal unit in the center. Slide-over chopping boards and draining racks can make practical use of the space when not in use.

Round sinks are not very popular in kitchens because they do not make the best use of the space available, although they can be a good second sink for vegetable preparation. Another rarity, but one that can be useful in an awkward corner area, is the triangular sink. The triangular cabinet usually has two sinks set in a diamond shape with the draining board in the triangular space at the top between the two.

Integral sinks are made of the same material as the countertop, Corian® for example, but for stand-alone sinks, steel is still universally popular. As with a steel counter, it is best to buy the thickest steel you can for a sink, preferably around $\frac{1}{16}$ inch thick, which will be strong, with less give and less noisy than a thinner steel sink. Finish is important, too. Steel sinks come in a satin finish, which is matte, and a high polish, which is more likely to show up scars and scratches.

Opposite **Plumbing faucets with an adjustable spout above the sink allows unhindered access.**
Top left **A good draining surface that leads directly into the sink is an important feature.**
Top right **Lever faucets are easy to operate with greasy or soapy hands.**
Right **The sink or sinks should be situated within the heart of the working area.**

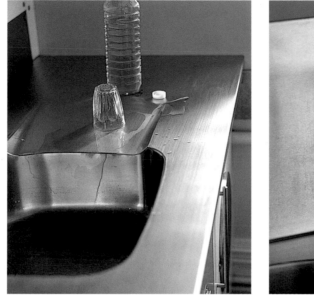

Ceramic sinks are also manufactured, and they are very popular in such setting as Traditional and Simple Country kitchens. Original, large, angular ceramic sinks can sometimes be found in antique shops and flea markets, although modern copies are easier to track down. Porcelain-enameled sinks with a cast-iron base come in various sizes and colors with a glossy enamel finish. These sinks are attractive and hardwearing, but may stain and chip if a hard item is dropped onto the surface. Granite, marble, and stone sinks can also be found but are rare and usually made to order.

Nonintegral sinks have to be mounted into the work surface, and there are a number of ways to approach this. Self-rimming sinks are finished with a rolled edge which can be set directly into the opening in the counter and sealed with a waterproof edge. Under-mounted sinks are usually installed into stone or solid counters, so the hard counter has a smooth, polished, or finished edge and the sink is placed directly beneath.

Faucets and spouts

There is a wide variety of faucets and spouts available and the best way to decide what you want is to analyze how you use them, what feels most comfortable in your hands, and which style seems appropriate to the look of your kitchen. There are very sophisticated combinations available, from those that are hands-free, turned on and off by breaking an infrared beam, to others that offer a

Opposite, clockwise from top left **This shallow, sloping sink is an integral part of the counter. A freestanding faucet in a utility area of the kitchen is useful for filling buckets and large vases. A stainless-steel sink is recessed neatly below a wooden counter. Double sinks are useful for busy kitchens. Cleaning agents are best stored under the sink, well away from food stuffs. The shape of the sink is a personal choice, but round bowls are unusual and attractive. Mixer faucets are always a popular choice. An extendable hose that pulls out of the main faucet can be used to direct a powerful jet of water. A hose is also useful for washing the surfaces around the sink.**

Above **Lever faucets can be turned on accidentally so it is important to turn them off properly.**

Far left **Sinks are often placed in front of a window so daylight can provide illumination.**

Left **A large and small sink may suit your needs better than two large ones.**

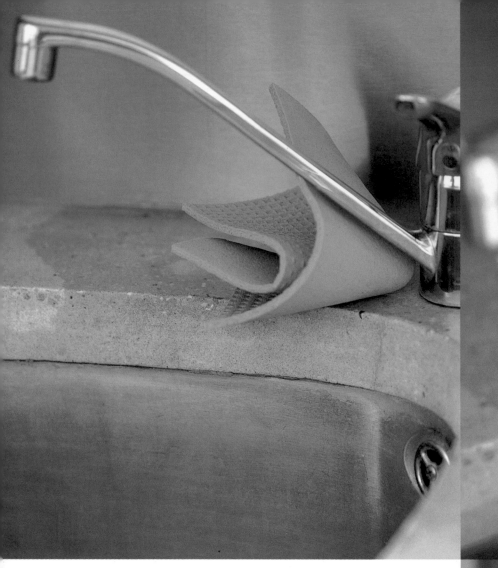

Above left to opposite right **Mixer faucets are**
popular because you can get just the right
temperature of water directly from one spout;
individual spouts keep the water temperature
separate, only to be mixed when it hits the sink.
A tall spout means you can fill tall pots and buckets easily, and it sits above the immediate work
area, where you might accidentally knock a
glass or china plate against it. It is important the
faucets and levers have a smooth and easy-to-
grip finish. Use steel wool for cast-iron pots and
pans, but avoid using it directly on stainless steel
surfaces since it may scratch.

Right **The shape of the spout is a personal**
choice; this arching curve has a pleasing line.

Far right **The plumbing in this work station is left**
deliberately exposed as a style feature. It also
has the advantage of being easily accessible
should a leak or blockage occur.

pull-out spout with brush and variable water pressure options. This installation looks attractive and exciting, but it may be an unnecessary luxury if you use the dishwasher every day and buy preprepared vegetables.

To assess grip and general tactile qualities, it is best to have a hands-on trial of the faucet. For those who suffer with hand mobility problems or who do a lot of baking, lever faucets are a good option. They are easy to turn on with a forearm or elbow, whereas a grip-and-turn faucet will become covered with ingredients, making it difficult to manipulate and to clean later. But check that your local building code allows for home installation of these industrial-design faucets—they can be wasteful of water.

The classic lines of a standard spout will suit most styles of kitchen. If possible, get an adjustable spout so you can direct the water into the corners of the sink for easy cleaning. A gooseneck spout has a more acute angle of curve and is longer and slenderer than the standard design. It is not a good idea for a busy sink since the flow produces a narrow jet of water, but it can be attractive in a low-use sink in a Traditional-style kitchen.

Faucets and spouts come in a number of finishes, including chrome, brass, colored epoxy coating, pewter, and nickel. Chrome is most popular, and it is available in matte, brushed, and high-polish finishes. It can easily be buffed up and made to sparkle with a dry soft cloth and is hardwearing and durable. Brass can be attractive, but make sure it is lacquered or finished with an epoxy seal; otherwise, you will have to spend time cleaning and polishing the faucets and spout. Finishes seal in the shine and take away the effort of maintenance. Epoxy coatings are applied over the metal base and fired at high temperatures to fix them. These finishes come in many colors, but simple white is most popular and least obtrusive.

Filters and disposal systems

If you installing a new sink, you might like to add an integral water filter that will purify the cold water as it passes through the system. If you use a lot of water for drinking or cooking, having a filter built in to the faucet can save a lot of time and bother of filling up filter units. There are various types of filters on the market, but basically the standard fixture has a filter installed under the sink that decontaminates.

Many people find a waste disposal unit a useful feature in a sink system, so that vegetable and smaller items of biodegradable matter can be readily and easily disposed of, saving time and the effort of taking out the trash. Also the instant disposal of waste that may decay saves rotting and unpleasant smells, especially during hot summer periods. In some cities, such as New York, it is technically illegal to install a waste disposal unit because the authorities prefer waste matter to be removed and disposed of by the authorities rather than mulched and sent through the sewage system.

Dishwashers

Modern machines have reconfigured interiors with racks and shelving systems that allow space for larger and bulkier loads, and built-in convection driers that circulate hot air, causing moisture to evaporate—quicker and more effective than older methods.

Dishwashers with two spray arms, one at the top and the other at the bottom, are often recommended because they ensure good overall distribution of water. At the bottom of

Below **Faucets placed at the side allow better access to a small sink.**
Right **The sink is a traditional one but the modern faucet and spout are simple enough to blend well.**
Below right **Even if you have a dishwasher, it is a good idea to have some draining space for washing the odd cup and glass.**
Opposite **In a large sink use a small bowl to save water.**

most machines is a filter, which catches larger particles of food. This should be cleaned regularly .

Many dishwashers can now be concealed behind panels. Cabinets with the control panel on the inner rim of the door are more suitable. These concealed controls mean that the outer door can be flush with other cabinet doors.

Stainless-steel interiors cope well with the heat and stress of high-power washes, but some metals, such as silver, will tarnish in reaction to the steel, so it is best to handwash silver or silver-plate flatware.

Check how quiet the machine is when in operation; there is nothing worse than being kept awake after a dinner party or trying to hold a phone conversation in competition with the spraying and whirring of the dishwasher. Most modern machines are reasonably quiet because manufacturers use more effective insulation.

appliances

Opposite **Refrigerators are growing in size and importance. Many come in a selection of colors and shapes designed to make them an integral part of the overall kitchen plan rather than a stand-alone object.**

Top left **Halogen rings with a smooth glass cover are simple to wipe clean when they cold.**

Top right **A combination of ovens with different facilities offers plenty of choice.**

Above left **Within a stove you can have gas jets and griddle facilities.**

Above right **Washing machines and other equipment can be concealed behind cabinet doors.**

Modern appliance are now designed not only to be efficient and attractive; increasingly manufacturers are responding to cultural demands and taking environmental issues on board. They are producing more machines that are energy saving or efficient and low in, if not free of, products such as chloro-florocarbons (CFCs). Before choosing your appliances—especially stoves —check what sort of power is available. While there will be no problem with electricity supply, it is possible you may not have a natural gas supply outlet in your kitchen. If

this is the case, you will have to call in a registered installer, which will add to the overall cost of the appliance.

Stoves

There are a number of combinations for power. For example, dual power, which offers natural gas burners and a self-cleaning electric oven, is very popular. Another popular feature in an electric oven is the convection fan: this circulates the heat evenly so each shelf or rack maintains the same level of heat. This is useful if you are baking several racks of cakes—there is no need to open the oven door and move the racks up and down. Also, if you are cooking several dishes with different flavors, such as a meatloaf and a fruit pie, the flavors will not mingle or taint the other dishes.

Natural gas ovens also offer a wide variety of modern features, such as an infrared broiler that can achieve temperatures of up to 1500 degrees, which will quickly sear food, replacing the standard broiler and barbecue-style grills.

Appliances evolve and are upgraded on a regular basis, and this can be seen in burners. Electric and gas burners used to be the norm, but new types of heat sources have changed the appearance and efficiency of the stovetop. Gas is still popular both in the traditional removable rack burner and the sealed burner. The sealed unit is marginally more expensive but easier to clean. Choose gas burners with an electric pilot light ignition—it means you don't have to relight the pilot when it goes out, and is safer than using matches.

Ceramic and glass burner tops are easy to clean and among the sleekest looking. The smooth top means that bits of food do not fall down between the rings and niches, and although fragile looking, the glass is tough and resilient. This type of stovetop can be heated by radiant, halogen, or magnetic induction coils. Magnetic induction is most similar to gas since it can be adjusted from high to low almost instantly.

Electric coil rings are most traditional. The electric heating element can be simply the exposed coiled rings, which glow when hot, or the rings can be concealed or integrated into metal plates that diffuse the heat. Natural gas rings are often favored over electric because of the greater control over heat and flame.

Left **A shelf under the burners holds pot holders and towels where they are easily accessible.**
Below left **The more small, complicated parts there are on a stove, there more there is to clean.**
Below **Large refrigerators have integral ice-making and cold drink facilities.**
Opposite **This stovetop combines a hot plate, gas burners, and a griddle.**

When choosing the configuration of your stove opt for a variety of ring strengths. Thermal heat is measured in British thermal units, known as BTUs. The higher the number, the more intense the heat, so a 600 BTU rating will simmer milk while 12,000 BTUs will boil water and heat woks.

New accessories have been developed to make the professional range more suitable for home cooking. For example, the old-fashioned raised grill that was difficult to balance a large pot on can be replaced with a closed grill plate and a special cradle to accommodate woks.

There are hundreds of types of stove, from the industrial-style freestanding version and the household adaptations of it, to the Victorian-style range. Traditional-style ranges now run mostly on oil, natural, or butane gas, or they can be adapted to run on electricity. They operate on a heat storage principal; the ovens and hot plates have thermostatically controlled temperatures. The cast-iron

lining to the lids and ovens are self-cleaning, as spillages and deposits of food burn off, leaving only ash behind. These stoves are heavy and require a level ground and an outside flue for ventilation. They can also be linked to the central heating system, but in the summer when you may need to turn the stove off you could need an alternative means of cooking.

Microwaves

Countertop microwaves can be a great asset to busy working people and families with a small baby or a number of children who need their meals served promptly and at differing times. As food is generally taken from the refrigerator or freezer and then placed in the microwave, it makes sense to position it near these appliances. Do not place the mircowave next to other machines that generate heat, such as a wall-mounted oven, as the heat may affect the microwave's performance. Also, if

the microwave is mounted on the wall or installed in a cupboard, make sure there is ventilation for the machine. When buying a microwave, look for features such as an extra shelf for simultaneous heating. And do not forget to check your dishes before using them. Are they microwave safe?

Exhaust hoods and fans

Do not skimp on a ventilation unit; not only will it remove smells and steam but in the process it will keep the temperature of the kitchen bearable and the atmosphere pleasant to work and eat in.

The size and strength of the ventilation system will depend on the floor area and capacity of the kitchen and the amount and type of cooking you do. If you only boil water twice a day and cook using a microwave, then a powerful fan is unnecessary. The strength of an exhaust fan is gauged in cubic feet per minute, abbreviated as CFM. Check with the supplier that the ventilator is strong enough for your needs.

Above **Beware of sharp edges on overhead furniture such as an exhaust fan.**
Right and far right **In a kitchen that has other functions, such as a living or dining area, an effective exhaust fan is essential not only to remove cooking smells but also to reduce condensation and smoke. Some fans have filters that use charcoal or a similar purifying agent, which may have to be changed or replaced, so make sure that access to the filter area is unhindered.**

Opposite **The distance between the burners and exhaust fan should be carefully calculated to achieve maximum efficiency. If possible it should be installed high enough so that you do not knock your head against it.**
Left **Fan-assisted ovens circulate hot air, which will cook food more quickly than a conventional oven.**
Below left **Make sure the sides of cabinets or cupboards close to a stove or an area where a naked flame is exposed are clad with a heat-resistant covering.**

There are two main types of ventilation system. One is the updraft hood that is positioned over the stove and sucks the steam, and with it the odors, away from the pots and pans as it rises. Updraft exhaust fans should be ducted through an outside wall or up a chimney so the moisture and smells are properly dispersed. This type of hood should be carefully positioned: if it is too close to the stove the steam may waft out on either side of the hood; if it is too far away the steam will disperse before reaching it. To check that the vent is well positioned—ideally about 30 inches above the stove—simply boil a pan of water and watch the vapor rise to the vent or place a sheet of paper on the unlit burners and see if it rises when the vent is turned on. Updraft systems are normally cased in a hood. The hood can be tailored to match the cabinets or be made into a feature by giving it a casing that contrasts with the rest of the room, such as copper or brushed steel. In contemporary kitchens the hood can be a sculpted feature and a focal point of the room, following the idea that if it is a large feature, make the most of it rather than trying to hide it.

The other type of ventilation system is the downdraft, which is generally a vent arrangement built into the back of the stovetop or island unit. This type of system is less obtrusive than a hood but not as effective, since it filters and recirculates the air rather than expelling it.

Exhaust fans such as the updraft and downdraft, as well as those installed directly into a wall or window, can be noisy, so ask the supplier how intrusive the noise level will be. There are superquiet exhaust fans on the market; these have extra insulation, which tends to make them more costly.

Refrigerators and freezers

Consider the size of refrigerator you need. Do you require a large-capacity machine with ice-making and cold-water facilities or would a side-by-side combination of two smaller units suit your needs and the size and dimensions of your room better? Do not buy a huge upright refrigerator-freezer that will take up most of a tiny kitchen when a smaller version or a combination of machines may give you more valuable counter space.

Modern refrigerators and freezers are increasingly energy efficient, using less than half the power they did a decade ago. Many are now CFC-free designs that eliminate the harmful ingredients that damage the earth's ozone layer. Many refrigerators have zonal refrigeration, which means that within one

cabinet there are areas of different degrees of coolness—chill at the base, cool in the center, and cold on top. A labor-saving frost-free facility cuts out the task of defrosting the freezer manually; the machine is capable of regulating the humidity and temperature so there is no icy buildup.

Refrigerators and freezers that fit between cabinets in a built-in kitchen are generally shallower, around 24 inches deep, than the equivalent freestanding appliances, which are between 28 to 34 inches deep. The reason for this is because the built-in variety is reduced to be flush with the cabinets that surround it, whereas the freestanding refrigerator-freezer can stand away from cabinets or tables that surround it.

There is also an increased demand for custom-made panels to add to the front of built-in appliances so the fascia of the refrigerator blends in with the cabinets. Freestanding machines are generally chosen with a standard white, steel, or colored panel that will blend in with the main colors of the room rather than matching the style or finish of the rest of the cabinets.

In addition to the chilling, freezing, and cooling features of the conventional appliance, there are a number of recent innovations, such as a wine cooler and under-counter refrigerator drawers. The wine cooler can be a tall cellar-style cabinet or a smaller 60-bottle machine that fits under a counter and is the size of a standard 24-inch cabinet. As

well as wine, bottles of mineral water and soft drinks may also be stored there. Most of these appliances have a temperature dial and variable temperature zones so that the degree of coolness can be adjusted to suit the type of wine being stored or your personal taste.

Refrigerator drawers are ideal for keeping fruit and vegetables lightly chilled; they are perfect for island or peninsular cabinets. A single drawer may provide enough space—if not, two drawers can be installed one on top of the other to provide double the capacity and a variety of chill and cool settings.

Top, from left **If you enjoy entertaining, have a refrigerator solely for chilling beers, water, wine, vodka, and glasses. Heavy refrigerator-freezers should butt neatly to neighboring cabinets and be based on a plinth or finished with a kickplate so they do not have to be moved for cleaning. If you use a lot of fresh ingredients, a small freezer over a larger refrigerator is ideal.**

Above left **The refrigerator has largely taken over the role of the pantry.**

Above right **A glass-front section makes it easy to see what is in stock.**

Opposite **Adjustable shelves are convenient for storing tall or bulky items.**

accessories

Opposite **A Dualit toaster is a timeless classic. Many modern metal gadgets are treated with a protective film, which means they can be wiped rather than polished.**

Left **Some juicers are only for citrus fruits, while others will take vegetables, separating the juice from the fibers and seeds.**

Below left **A blender is ideal for making soups, mayonnaise, and milkshakes.**

Bottom left **Modern styling has improved the look of many utilitarian gadgets, such as toasters.**

Below **This manual citrus juicer is an attractive piece of equipment that can be left on display.**

Bottom right **This mixer is the up-to-date version of an old favorite. It is sturdy and durable, and the whisks are interchangeable to suit tasks from beating egg whites to kneeding dough.**

In addition to large-scale appliances there is a vast array of smaller machines, tools, utensils, and gadgets available that make a cook's working life easier and more fun. Machines should be carefully chosen, primarily for their use and function, but also for their good looks. Apparatus that is going to be left out on the counter should be attractive and contribute to the overall appearance of the room. Less attractive but nonetheless vital and useful pieces of machinery should be stored in drawers and cupboards.

Any items that are used frequently should be stored on the surface or kept adjacent to the work surface. Other machines that are heavy to move can be left on the surface under a cover to camouflage their bulk and protect the machine from steam and grease. If it is a machine that is rarely used, it could perhaps be stored elsewhere and brought into the kitchen when needed, thereby freeing up vitally needed storage space.

Countertop machines

When choosing these smaller appliances, try running through an imaginary day. For example, on rising the first task is breakfast. Do you drink juice from a carton or do you prepare it fresh? If so, would an easy hand-lever non-electrical squeezer do or would a small electric juicer be better? Consider how much time you have to wash and dry the gadget after use, and decide whether the machine and its accessories should be dishwasher-safe.

What is your regular hot drink—cappuccino, espresso, instant coffee, tea, or hot water with lemon? For cappuccino and espresso a specific machine is the quickest and most effective option. A toaster offers the speediest way of toasting English muffins or bread, but if you have more time the broiler will do the same job.

After breakfast, consider other meals and their preparation as an aid to selecting additional equipment. A blender is useful for making lunchtime soups and may be combined with an attachable gadget for grinding coffee beans or nuts. These facilities may be offered as part of a food processor, but if you make soup on a regular basis, the blender may be easier to use and to wash. A food processor can be bulky and difficult to clean, and it may be better replaced with a selection of smaller individual machines.

Top, from left **This modern round-bodied kettle sits snugly and safely on the trivet over a gas burner. A basic old-fashioned cast-iron kettle has a traditional charm. Steel pans can be expensive, but they will last a lifetime and will not taint or affect food as aluminum pans can.**

Above, from left **Choose the right size equipment to suit your needs—this simple filter makes coffee for one a quick and easy business. Heat-resistant glass is now used for many items of cookware; this glass teapot brings a new look to a classic vessel. There are few things more welcoming than the smell of fresh coffee brewing, and this stove-top percolator will ensure a ready supply.**

Opposite **In this modern streamlined kitchen the utensils on display are all suitably good looking. But if you hang utensils on the backplate you must take care when reaching across for them when the burners are in use.**

If you are an avid fan of Oriental cuisine, an electric rice steamer is a boon, and for grinding herbs and spices for these dishes a pestle and mortar is essential. Salad lovers may find a vegetable spinner useful for getting excess water out of lettuce and other leaves. Pasta fans might favor a pasta maker and cutter. Bread makers that knead the dough are also labor saving but tend to be bulky, while yogurt makers are popular once again with the renewed interest in healthy eating.

Basic equipment

Standard kitchen equipment should include a good selection of pots and pans for various types and amounts of cooking. Aluminum pans may cause certain foods to discolor or taint the flavor. Stain-less steel is light and durable, and copper, though expensive, is a good conductor of heat and attractive to display. Copper pans are good for sauces and flambéd dishes. Cast-iron casseroles and pans are heavy but good for slow cooking and are perfect for cooking on a range.

Skillets are another basic piece of equipment. Nonstick linings make them easier to use and to wash. Ideally a skillet should not be too heavy, since you should be able to lift it easily and move it on and off the heat as you need to.

Wok cooking has become increasingly popular: it requires little fat and cooks noodles, vegetables, and other ingredients quickly. Some woks come with domed lids that keep juices and steam inside the pan, making the food moist and succulent.

There are many other specialized pots and pans, such as asparagus boilers and fish kettles, but they are ancillaries and not essential to the basic kitchen battery.

However, good-quality sharp knives are an essential. Carbon-steel blades have to be carefully dried and cared for as they are prone to rust spots, but they last indefinitely and can be easily sharpened. Ordinary stainless-steel blades will not rust, but they may be more difficult to sharpen. All knives should be stored with care, preferably in a block or a rack, both to avoid cut fingers and to keep blades sharp. Magnetic holders that can be screwed to a wall near a work surface are also good. Using a sharpening steel—a long, textured rod on a handle—is the easiest and quickest way to revitalize the edge of a blade, but if you are not used to using a steel, ask someone in a reputable kitchen equipment store to show you how it is done, because there is a knack to it.

Strainers, colanders, and slotted spoons are useful for separating food from fluids, whether they be water, broth, or sauce. Wooden spoons and spatulas are best used for stirring and are preferable for use in enamel or nonstick pots because the wood will not scratch or damage the finish. A pancake turner is designed for turning and lifting flat foods as well as longer fish and meat or cakes, as it gives good leverage and a flat support. Ladles and large spoons with long handles will enable you

Above **For crushing dried herbs and spices, an old-fashioned pestle and mortar cannot be faulted.**

Far left **A good sharp knife is essential and a collection of different sizes and types of knives allows you to choose the right tool for the job, but sharp blades should be carefully stored. This magnetic knife rack holds the blades in place, leaving the handles free.**

Left **Weighing scales are useful in the kitchen. They come in many guises—this one has a traditional appearance.**

Left **The lip on this chopping board prevents it from sliding across the surface when it is used.**
Below **Wood is thought to have antiseptic qualities which makes it ideal for chopping boards.**
Bottom, from left **Pitchers are indispensable in the kitchen as measuring aids, for serving drinks, and for displaying flowers. Reinforced glass will not absorb pungent food smells and can be washed with boiling water. Various sizes and types of knives are needed for different tasks.**

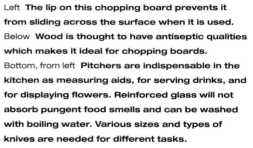

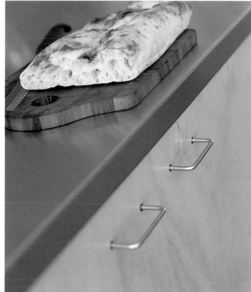

to stir hot dishes at a distance from the heat source and to take larger quantities of broth or sauce out of a container. A large fork, again with a long handle, will make prodding and turning roasts easier. Graters, from small for nutmeg to large for cheese and bread crumbs, are an invaluable tool, and will also give a more professional finish to food preparation.

Weighing scales are useful not just for gauging cake ingredients but also for weighing dried ingredients such as beans and pasta to make sure you get the right quantity. Because some recipes require spoon and cup measurements it is essential that you have a set of specifically calibrated spoons and a set of measuring cups.

Waste disposal

Waste disposal is a major part of life in the kitchen—with more and more packaging and pre-prepared foods the trash can seems to fill ever more rapidly. Also, with a strong cultural move toward recycling and organic gardening, waste is more frequently divided into different lots so that each type can be sent to the right end. For example, a small can for fruit and vegetable peelings, egg shells, and other biodegradable matter can be taken directly to a compost heap. Aluminum cans, flattened by stamping on them or with a mechanical press, can be recycled. Glass can also be separated out—some recycling depots require it to be divided into brown, green, and white—for reuse, as can newspapers, magazines, and printed paper waste.

Top right Storing pots with their lids makes it simpler to pair them up.
Right Old-fashioned meat hooks are efficient, movable hangers.
Far right Having whisks and ladles near the stove saves time and effort.
Below Keep pans within easy reach.
Below right Metal utensils are hardwearing.
Opposite, clockwise from left A good-size trash can is essential for bulky waste. Individual recycling cans hold wet and dry waste separately. Pedal-operated flip-top trash cans are useful when your hands are full.

cabinets

The kitchen is a fully functioning work station, and the day-to-day activity of cooking and producing meals generates a huge amount of gear, from tools and utensils to plates and cups and, of course, the raw material—food. All of this equipment must be stored in a systematic and organized way so you can locate what you need quickly and access it easily. Storage is the primary function of the main furniture in the kitchen—the cabinets. But there are other considerations when choosing cabinets than merely containing all your clutter: storage cannot dominate the room to such an extent that there is insufficient space left for the food preparation itself, and because they are such an important feature in the room, the cabinets must look good and work well with the appliances you have chosen.

Not all cabinets need to be new or built in. A freestanding kitchen is an ideal place to use a mix of old and new pieces of furniture. An old chest of drawers can be used for linen and lightweight storage and an armoire or cabinet for larger items. With this style of layout, cabinets of all shapes and sizes can be brought together to form useful storage and work areas. Small pieces can be jacked up on pedestals or bases so they form a level surface with other furniture, and, if required, a countertop can be laid over a number of such cabinets to create a continuous solid work area and to prevent bits of food and crumbs from falling down between the individual cupboards.

Cabinet layout

Cabinets can be installed in a number of ways. The simplest is a straight row of cupboards top and bottom, but to add interest and variety the wall cabinets could be staggered so that some are higher than others. For example, over an area of countertop where small appliances and machines

Opposite **Shelves can be subdivided with small internal racks to give extra storage areas.**
Left, clockwise, from top left **A butcher block-trolley provides additional work surface on wheels as well as useful storage. Cabinets near or above open flames should be lined or faced with a heat protective fascia. Even ingredients and dried foods can be attractive if well displayed. A variety of internal drawers and shelves can be useful. Where possible, store items close to the point where they will be used. Glass-front cabinets allow decorative items to be put on show.**

Cabinets 139

are used, the cabinets could be lower (but still giving easy access to the work surfaces), making it
easy to get machines in and out of the cabinets.
Where the cabinets are to be used for storing items
that are seldom used, they could be placed higher
up on the wall. But this staggered effect needs to
be carefully planned so it looks balanced and pur-
poseful rather than random and accidental.

Among a wall of solid-doored cabinets it can be
a relief to have a series of open shelves. The
shelves can be used to display cookbooks, attractive gadgets, or china, but open shelves are best
sited away from the stove where steam and grease
may cause damage to books and grime to accumulate on china. Under-cabinet shelves can be useful
places for attractive stainless-steel or enamel
cookware to be shown off. The tools will be readily
accessible and they will add color and interest
among a run of cabinets.

In addition to shelves, plate and wine racks can
be used to interrupt the line of cabinets. In a small
kitchen a plate rack for drying and storing dishes
could be placed above a sink and between two
upper wall-mounted cabinets. Otherwise, it could
be positioned over the counter and be an attractive
as well as practical storage feature. Wine racks are
often built into residual or leftover space where
built-in cabinets cannot be accommodated. These
wine racks are generally for show rather than serious use. They may house a dozen or so bottles of

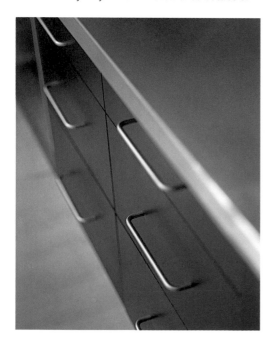

wine used for cooking rather than for serious drinking; the temperature of the kitchen will vary enormously, a less-than-ideal situation for maintaining quality wine in good condition.

Interior details

Within the cabinets you can install a number of useful interior fittings to divide the space available, such as drawer dividers and flatware trays (these can be standard or two-tiered with a sliding top layer and a rigid base that gives double capacity). Extra-deep pan drawers for storing large pans and their lids are often lined with ridged rubber mats that stop the pots and lids from sliding around and marking the drawer and can be easily removed and cleaned when they get grubby. When choosing these interior facilities, check they will be adjacent to the areas where the items they hold will be used.

Opposite, top **A range of drawer and cupboard storage is used as a base for this stovetop.**
Opposite bottom, from left **A mix of drawers and cupboards provides a variety of storage to cope with both small and large items. The cabinets used in the passageway adjoining the kitchen are in the same modern unadorned style, but a contrasting color is used to define the different rooms. Deep drawers, like those found in a filing cabinet, will hold more bulky items.**
Above **Reinforced and laminated glass can be used in most types of cupboard doors. Opaque glass will give the door a light appearance but conceal jumbled contents, whereas clear glass will allow an attractive or decorative arrangement to be part of the decor. Glass can also be patterned and decorated with sandblasting and etching techniques.**
Left **A steel rack with deep open mesh shelves and an opaque glass door is set into a recess in the wall, to make excellent inexpensive storage.**

If fruit and vegetables or other perishable goods are to be stored on racks or shelves they will keep for much longer if they have plenty of air circulating around them. If you rest them on hard, solid surfaces in closed drawers moisture from the fruit or vegetables will cause mold to form more readily. Wire-mesh drawers are a good option, as are natural wicker baskets. In both cases the open weave prevents moisture from accumulating. The main disadvantage is that small pieces of broken peel or soil may work their way through the open spaces and tumble

Opposite, top left **A cart is a useful accessory, especially in a large kitchen. It can be used to transport ingredients from one side of the room to another, and, if it is the right height, the top can also be used as additional work space.**

Opposite, top right **Items that are often used in tandem, such as mixing bowls, baking sheets, and cooling racks, are best stored together so they can be taken out at the same time.**

Opposite, bottom, from left **A series of small shelves in a tall cupboard leaves space to one side for taller items. Shallow drawers are best for flatware and linens so they are easily accessible. Cupboard fronts in different colors can make basic storage appear more interesting.**

Left **In cabinets or drawers where jam or other sticky jars or bottles are to be kept, a removable, washable base mat is advisable.**

Above **This cabinet façade hides a trash can, the lid of which is set into the counter.**

to the bottom of the cupboard or onto another shelf. A fine-mesh panel inserted between the drawers would collect this debris while still allowing a free flow of air. Wicker can also be hard to clean; wire mesh can simply be wiped with a damp cloth, but wicker will need a scrub with a hard-bristled brush.

Think about the construction of drawers and the type of runners you will need. For drawers that will hold lightweight items such as dish towels, table linen, or flatware, plastic runners are suitably smooth running and relatively inexpensive, but for drawers destined to hold cast-iron pots the runners should be sturdier. Metal is more costly than plastic, but it will withstand the pressures of a heavier load. Metal runners should run smoothly, but they may require a little lubrication if they become old and stubborn.

Top left **These wire-mesh trays prevent vegetables from becoming sweaty or moldy as they allow air to circulate freely around the produce.**

Top right **It is a good idea to put a heatproof layer of protection between an oven and a cabinet in which you are planning to store foodstuffs that might be affected by high temperatures.**

Above and right **Baskets make a change from solid drawers, and they can be lifted out to carry linens directly to the table. They would also be good for fruits and vegetables as, like mesh ones, they allow the contents to "breathe."**

Opposite **A good mix of wall and floor cabinets, open shelving, drawers, and mobile storage makes a hardworking and attractive kitchen.**

Too many drawers can be inefficient—you are limited by their size and shape as to what they will hold, and they may tempt you to fill them with unnecessary clutter—so analyze exactly where you will need them and what you will keep in them. You may find that a single five-drawer unit and one or two cabinets with drawers above open cupboard space is enough. Many items such as flatware and linen for formal dinners could be stored elsewhere, leaving space in the kitchen for essentials.

Beneath the cabinet doors is the area where the kickboard is situated. In most kitchens, this board finishes the cabinets and links them to the floor, hiding the legs or supports underneath the cabinet and preventing dirt from finding its way into spaces that are awkward to clean. But in a small kitchen where space is really precious, this area can be used to house a number of small drawers that can be used to store skillets and other less bulky pieces of kitchen equipment.

Cupboard doors

The contents of a cabinet need not necessarily be standard storage. Cupboard doors can be used to conceal what goes on behind them and to put a good face on something that is not attractive. For example, to maintain the flow of cabinets and to give overall symmetry to a kitchen, a fake door panel can disguise a trash can or a washing machine, and a mock drawer front could hide a

Above **An unusual wedge-shaped hanging rack projects items on the upper rungs, making it easier to select and remove objects. The depth and size of items can be graduated from the top down so the area directly in front of the stove is not obscured or hindered by large pots or pans, and items used most often are close at hand.**
Top right **Drawers do not have to be square: these rounded metal-mesh drawers create an softer edge to the overall façade and bring a different texture and finish into the plan.**
Right **Bits may fall through the mesh drawer, so a layer of wire screen is used to make a sliding lid for the drawer below.**

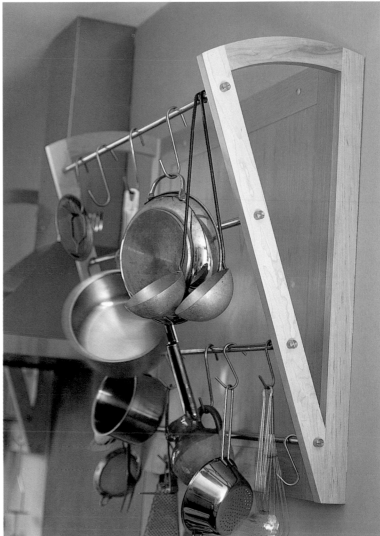

pull-out extension table or chopping board. A solid door, whether it is made of wood, laminate, or composition board, is the most useful option for creating a range of versatile storage like this, as you are not limited to what you can store behind it.

However, having a kitchen furnished completely with solid doors can look heavy and clumsy. Having just one or two cupboards with glazed doors will not pose too many restrictions on your storage arrangements, because there will always be some objects in the kitchen that are attractive enough to be displayed. Decorative and clear, or opaque and sandblasted, glass panels can be an interesting addition to a kitchen, adding light to a dark or small room. With improvements in safety and the development of reinforced and laminated types, glass is now suitable for general use.

Top left **Keep fragile items stored together and heftier, more robust objects in another place; mixing china and cast-iron pots in the same drawer will lead to breakages.**

Above **Metal equipment can benefit from being stored over a warm area such as a stove because the rising heat will help to dry out any moisture left after washing, but unless they are used frequently they will gather grease and dust.**

Left **Narrow spaces can be utilized with pull-out racks like this one. They can be used for keeping condiments and spices or cleaning materials.**

furniture

The furniture in a kitchen caters to the subsidiary functions of the room: dining and, to a lesser extent, relaxing. Stools, tables, and chairs in a kitchen may be informal, but they should be chosen to complement the overall style of decoration. The furniture may revolve around a selection of colors in the same design or comprise a mix of styles with a similar theme—say, using the same materials, such as wood or chrome. Old and new pieces can often be mixed successfully. It may not be necessary to have matching stools and chairs; in fact, different styles of furniture could help to delineate between the informal kitchen and the more structured dining area. For example, in a kitchen with a breakfast bar area high stools will be the most appropriate seating, but around a table in the same room where more formal dining may take place the seating will more likely be provided by chairs.

Comfortable chairs are a must if you expect friends and family to sit around a table and take time over a meal. The chairs should be the right height for the table so you do not have to lean over or stretch up to a plate, and there should be enough room to cross your legs and relax after dining. If the chairs are hard, wood or steel say, you may need to add a pad or cushion. Although they can be less attractive, molded plastic chairs tend to have more "give" and are easy to wipe clean and maintain in a sticky and greasy environment.

Opposite **If a seat is to be used for dining, and will have to support someone for hours at a time, then it should be comfortable. This woven webbing will be more relaxing to sit on than a chair with a hard wooden or solid plastic seat.**
Right **In this minimal monochrome room the color and style of the chairs is the focal point.**

Above **Two fifties-style chairs give a period feel to a timeless kitchen. Stools can be used for quick snacks at the breakfast bar, but the two upholstered armchairs offer more long-term comfort.**

Right **A stool or high chair is ideal for a breakfast-bar area that may be used from the other side as a counter for food preparation.**

Far right **The back on this stool gives support and makes it more relaxing to linger on for a second cup of coffee. The padded seat also adds to the comfort factor.**

Opposite **These classic chrome-and-polished-wood stools would look good in any style of kitchen. The curved back leg and small crossbar add interest.**

Right and far right **A mix of modern and classic designs furnishes the dining area of this kitchen. Curved bentwood chairs are an old but continually popular style. They are both lightweight and attractive. The stump-legged stool is a modern design, while the chrome-and-red table is reminiscent of 1950s diners. All work well with the decor of the kitchen.**

Below **An angular dining table echoes the straight lines of the archway that links the kitchen to the dining area as well as to the dark rectangular window frames. Solid chunky chairs add substance with their shape and an injection of color.**

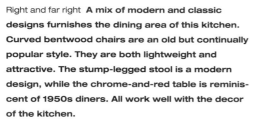

When choosing high stools for a breakfast bar think of comfort. For example, if the stool does not have a rung or footrest on the base of the legs, your legs may get tired from dangling around in the air, so it may be wise to add a footrail onto the side of the bar or to find a suitable stool that has a rail incorporated in its design. In general, stools can also be taxing on the back. It is more relaxing to have some form of lower lumbar support, although this comfort may have to be sacrificed if the stool is to be stored under a counter.

Tables come in all sorts of shapes and sizes and they should be chosen to suit the rest of the furnishings in the room as well as in a size and dimension that is appropriate. All tables in kitchen areas should be easy to wipe clean. If the area is small or serves more than one purpose, a drop-leaf table may be useful, so that the table can remain compact when not in use and elongated for dining or food preparation for a large gathering. When choosing a table beware of buying one with too many or badly positioned legs. The legs may look like an attractive feature in the shop but think of the practicalities of seating six or eight people around it, and consider that someone may have to sit astride the legs during such a gathering. For small kitchens, look at the possibilities of foldaway furniture. Some small tables can be attached to the wall and let down flush with the wall when not in use. Chairs that fold flat can be stored in a cupboard or in another room, to be brought out when needed.

Whatever furniture you choose, make sure that it is suitable for a kitchen environment, in particular that it can be easily cleaned. Grand padded chairs with fabric upholstery will soon be stained or splashed in this busy room.

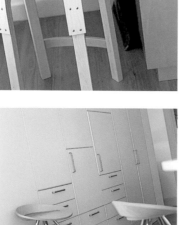

Above, above right, and right **It may be easier to buy the stool and then adjust the height of the counter, rather than trying to find stools to accommodate the counter height.**
Top right **Classic fine beechwood chairs like these are flexible enough to offer comfort.**
Far right and opposite below **A table with adjustable extra leaves is a bonus when entertaining friends.**
Opposite above **A large upholstered sofa defines where the kitchen area ends and the living area begins.**

display

Decoration can be applied to a kitchen in many ways: there does not need to be a great riot of frills, patterns, and artifacts for there to be embellishment—in fact, unnecessary clutter will only attract grease and grime and add to the task of cleaning. Utilitarian and simple objects can be attractive if they are well ordered. In Simple Modern and New Professional kitchens gilt-framed pictures, fancy curtains, and ornate china will look out of place, yet decoration can be included as long as the items are in keeping with their surroundings.

For example, in a minimalist kitchen a glass shelf of strictly regimented glasses can be interesting, and immaculate chrome canisters will also be eye catching. Glass shelves give a feeling of lightness, as though the objects on them were floating rather than set solidly, as they appear on a wooden shelf. But when there are only a few items on show they have to be perfect, clean, and polished. If there is little to attract the eye elsewhere they become the focus of attention. A directional spotlight can be used to highlight simple displays, such as a row of glasses, when the rest of the room is illuminated by low-level light. Or, if the display is placed near a window, it will be illuminated by daylight, which will accentuate the sparkle and reflections on the glass.

Opposite **Simple everyday items can look attractive if well displayed.**
Top left **Shiny items such as chrome canisters should be sparkling, not smudged with greasy finger marks.**
Above **Polished glassware is always appealing.**
Left **Choose items to put on show that are appropriate to the overall theme or scheme of the kitchen.**

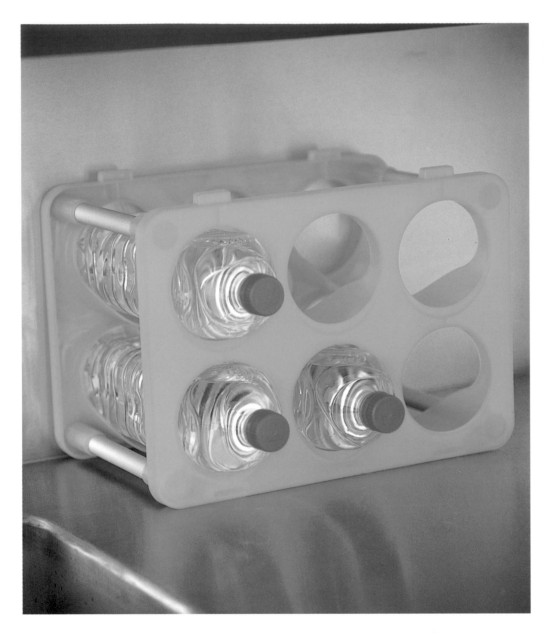

Above **In a plain or monotone scheme, a single bright object like this vivid plastic bottle rack will become a focal point.**
Top right **A single unexpected item or object can attract the eye.**
Above right **A glass shelf makes the objects on it appear to be suspended in the air.**
Opposite **Soften a clinical steel façade with a single bloom.**

When placing objects in groups on a shelf it can be interesting to split them into clusters of three or five—somehow groups of odd-number items look more interesting than groups of even numbers of objects. White plates on a plate rack can be grouped so that the different sizes of plates create a pattern: a group of dinner plates followed by a similar number of side plates, a few more dinner plates, and then some bowls, for example.

A single unexpected item among a line of compatible objects can also be appealing. For example, a colored glass among a row of plain glasses, a wicker whisk in a line of metal pancake turner. The juxtaposition of a simple curved vase against a

background of angular knives or cabinet doors will also be of interest in a room where there is little other decoration.

Fresh fruits and vegetables, the very ingredients of meals to be cooked, can in themselves be decorative objects. A dark wood bowl filled with polished red apples, a wicker basket laden with speckled brown eggs, bottles of oil with chiles or herbs suspended in the rich yellow green liquid are all appealing and appropriate to the location.

Storage containers can also be attractive—a brightly colored plastic wine rack will bring order to a jumble of wine bottles and its color and shape may be pleasing. Wire or wicker baskets filled with

comestibles can also be left on display. Flatware, shiny and silvery, can be made to appear inviting and interesting if stored in an old wooden tray or in bundles in pots or jars. Old knives and forks with ornate handles or polished yellow bone handles can be stored blade down so that the handles splay out like the bones of a fan.

Traditional and Simple Country kitchens are more suited to arrangements of plates and china, especially on hutches or open shelves. In fifties-style kitchens old enamelware and early Denby china are appropriate—the simple classic lines of enameled plates, bowls, and pitchers are pleasing to the eye and the decorative china will help emphasize the theme and period of the decor.

Country style need not be cluttered but it does encourage the spirit of industry and collecting—jars of homemade jellies and pickles, bunches of dried herbs over the hearth or fireplace. Pillows on old wooden chairs, and gingham tablecloths and napkins add softness and comfort. But a little can go a long way—too many baskets and bunches of flowers, rows of china bowls, and heaps of baking trays may make it look as though you are running a store rather than an efficient and hygienic kitchen.

Where the displays are arranged is important. If the items are frequently used, like glasses and tableware, then they can be left on open shelves because they will be in and out of the dishwasher or sink regularly. Glass shelves are handsome but must be kept dust free, so a couple of them may be enough—a special feature rather than the norm. Cabinets with glass panels in the doors will allow items to be seen yet provide a barrier between them and the steam and smoke of the kitchen. Counter areas are really the hub of kitchen activity and should be kept as uncluttered and clean as possible, but a few good-looking items can be positioned to the back of the counter or in areas that are less frequently used.

It is an Oriental custom to have a small niche in the wall of the main living room, under which is kept a chest that contains the family's treasures. Each day a single treasure is taken out and displayed in the niche. The single item, a vase or bowl maybe, can then be appreciated without the distraction of other ornaments. This "less is more" philosophy can be applied to any plainly decorated room—even the kitchen.

Opposite, clockwise from top **Arrangements of goods in neat wire baskets create an appealing symmetry. Flatware old or new can be displayed.**

This page, clockwise from top left **Different shapes and sizes of the same item, such as gleaming copper pans sending out endless reflections of themselves, add architectural interest in an otherwise well-ordered room. A modern knife block with a graceful metal stand is an attractive and safe way of storing knives. Instead of having a motley collection of bags of flour and sugar, decant the contents into matching tins or jars. Open-shelf display is good for items that are used regularly. Even dishes on a drying rack can be pleasingly arranged. China shapes do not have to be identical—as long as they are of the same color they will sit happily together on a shelf. Uneven numbers of objects make interesting groups. Variety can bring interest: display utensils together in tall vases and glasses.**

dec

introduction

Decoration can be a way of reviving and revitalizing an existing kitchen and an opportunity to bring a more fashionable note to a classic or traditional setting. If you are starting from scratch, certain schemes and colorways may already have been suggested by the type and style of cabinets you have chosen to install. The size and shape of the room and the amount of natural light available may also influence your choice.

Decoration involves a number of different finishes and materials, from paints and ceramic tiles to soft furnishings such as drapes, shades, seat pillows, and tablecloths. To give the whole room a cohesive look it is wise to plan your decorative scheme throughout before putting paint on the wall or buying yards of fabric. As with the general planning of the layout of the kitchen, it is a good idea to keep a notebook of decorating ideas, into which you can staple samples of material, and keep color cards from paint manufacturers and photographs and clippings from magazines. If you are good at drawing you might also want to sketch in ideas that you see or imagine could be adapted to your setting. The book can also be used to keep a list of measurements handy, for example, for windows and floor areas, so that you can gauge the costs of materials when you chance upon something you like—this sort of comparison will help you keep an eye on your budget. This reference book will prove invaluable when you start to work out your look, whether you do it yourself or with the help of a professional decorator, as it is easier to show examples of a color or a fabric finish than it is to try to describe it in words.

The actual materials used for decorating will vary in type and availability of color. For example, the tough and efficient surfaces—the countertops, backsplashes, and floors—come in a more limited range of color than the paint for the wall. Therefore, when choosing the "colorful" parts of the look make sure they blend and sit comfortably with the less colorful but "useful" elements. Do not be too dogmatic or rigid about your selection, as you may be disappointed if you cannot track down just the right shade of bright green work surface. Remember too much of one color can be overpowering; try different shades of a color or contrast it with a brighter or darker color for variety. Look at texture as well. The types of material you might use—smooth ceramic tiles or opaque glass bricks—can be contrasted with roughly woven linen, brick, or grained wood. Various textures have different effects and the combination of smooth and rough can create visual interest in a plainly colored scheme.

Opposite **Choosing the decoration for your kitchen gives you the opportunity to explore an abundance of colors, textures, and materials.**

color

Colors for kitchens can be divided into four main groups. The first category is the cool spectrum of blue, green, gray; secondly there are the hot shades—red, orange, sunshine yellow; then the dramatic colors of crimson, deep purple, and black; and finally there are the pastels, a title that covers beige, soft pink, baby blue, and pale primrose yellow.

When mixing colors it is often useful to refer to the three primary colors: red, blue, and yellow. Using these colors as a base you can work out a safe combination for a scheme. For example, if you mix blue and yellow you get green, and as a basic rule of thumb blue, yellow, and green are compatible in something like a fabric print or a ceramic tile pattern. Red and yellow make orange, so again those three colors are likely to be harmonious, as are red, blue, and their offspring purple.

Using darker and lighter shades of a color can also be used to interesting effect and is often referred to by professional decorators as "tone on tone." For example, plain cabinets may be painted a medium gray; the kickboard, door frames, and the panel under the cabinets could be in medium charcoal, with a similar shade of granite for the counter; and the walls painted the faintest hint of pearl gray. A steel sink and drainer, silvery taps, and chrome accessories would all work well against this setting, but add unexpected splashes of color—such as a fuchsia-pink tablecloth, a row of bold terra-cotta-and-black ethnic

Opposite **Details are an important ingredient in the overall decoration: shining handles on a plain painted cabinet give a lift to its appearance.**
Above **Choose colors that are appropriate to the style or period of decoration you are following.**
Right **The color of a shelf or cabinet can act as a contrasting back-ground and can highlight the objects displayed on or in it.**
Far right **By painting a single piece of furniture in a different color from the walls you will make it stand out and give it more impact.**

plates, and jars or a couple of bright red enamel cooking pots—to prevent the whole thing from becoming bland or dull.

Lighting and color

The type of light used in the room can also change the appearance of a color. The intensity of the color often changes, depending on whether it is viewed in natural or artificial light, so, if possible, paint an area of wall with the color you have in mind or pin up a swatch of the fabric you propose to use for the shades or soft furnishings, and live with it through a day. Look at the colors in daylight, again at dusk, and then with artificial light. Dark colors become denser as the day progresses, so what might seem like a strong but interesting color on a bright summer morning may become gloomy and oppressive on a dark winter day. A sunny yellow paint may be great in daylight but become acidic or "dirty" in electric light. Also check fabrics and paints together, as what appears to be a good match in the fluorescent rays of a store's lighting fixture can look world's apart in daylight, or when you get them home. Blue lights, such as fluorescents, can have a dramatic effect on some of the more modern fluorescent or acid colors, so these shades should always be checked against other colors in the room and in the full range of light sources to be used in that room.

The way in which color is distributed is also important. A dark ceiling and pale walls will make the ceiling appear lower. Dark kickboards and a

Left **This kitchen is painted in a hot vivid orange that makes the stone-floored room seem warm even in the depth of winter. The original stone surround to the fireplace has been lined with steel and is used to house a modern professional-style stove and broiler.**

Top left **Although the color is contemporary, many of the objects displayed against it are traditional; the choice and arrangement of the items make old and new compatible.**

Top right and above **A rail of gleaming utensils and the chrome-and-glass storage jars are highlighted by the strong wall color.**

Opposite **The dark muted blue of the back wall accentuates the chrome exhaust pipe, clock, and pale paneled door.**

Below **The blue wall butts up to the white side walls and ceiling, chrome countertops, and pale sanded wood flooring, making a feature out of the darker expanse of wall.**

Right **A righ warm color like this yellow can brighten a dark or basement kitchen. It also suits darker shades of wood.**

Below right **White accessories look clean and fresh against the strongly colored walls.**

richly colored floor will make the floor appear closer. Darker painted details, such as door and window frames, against a pale wall or pale cabinets will make the details stand out, so if you are highlighting these features make sure they are of a quality and finish that will withstand scrutiny and are worthy of the accolade.

Structural emphasis

High ceilings and tall walls can be reduced by dividing the wall into different areas and painting them different colors. This technique works particularly well in period rooms. The ceiling can be painted in a medium tone, beneath that a picture rail can be added at about 2 feet from the top of the wall, and the area between the ceiling and the rail painted in white. The wall beneath the picture rail to the dado rail (which is at approximate hip height) can be painted in the same color as the ceiling. The dado

itself can be picked out with white paint and beneath that the wall can be painted a much deeper shade of the ceiling color. This division will help reduce the size of the room and also makes the room bright (with the white and pale colors) but the area where chairs, boots, and bags may scuff is dark and so less likely to show marks.

If the room is an uneven shape, perhaps as when an extention is added to an existing house or an apartment has been created by subdividing rooms, then using a variety of shades and colors on the different sections of the wall will not only add interest but may also help to even out the overall appearance. For example, if a wall has a recess you could choose to ignore it and paint it the same color as the rest of the walls, or you could paint it richer or brighter color and make it a point of interest. If the main walls are rich raspberry red, the recess could be painted in a harmonious shade of

Above **Mixing and matching colors can give a kitchen a more modern apearance. Bands of color travel down the walls, over units, and onto below-counter storage, forming a pattern of stripes.**

Above right **Painting the recesses of shelves in a range of colors in an otherwise monotone kitchen will make the shelves and their contents a focal point.**

Right **You could use color to denote the contents of various storage areas—green for vegetable steamers, red for frying pans, for example.**

Opposite **Different colors but in similar tones or strengths can sit comfortably side by side, as this vibrant mix demonstrates.**

reddish brown, giving a luxurious feel and creating a change of emphasis. Using a deeper shade than the main wall will also create the optical illusion that the recess is deeper, whereas painting it a lighter and brighter shade will make it appear more shallow.

Creating a style

The combination of color and style is very important, especially if you are following a particular look. For example, vivid orange and acid green are associated with a more contemporary range of colors and would look

out of place in a period kitchen, whereas New Professional or Simple Modern kitchens with clean stainless steel units and simple tiling can act as a foil to almost any color.

Another deciding factor may be that you have chosen a particular fabric for shades, seat cushions, or tablecloths. The colors within the pattern of the textile might give you a starting point for your decorative look. But do remember, if the room is small and dark, pale shades will make it look more spacious, so if the shades fabric is dark, choose a lighter tone of one of the dark colors.

Opposite **Rather than a color on the opposite end of the spectrum from steel's silvery-gray tones, this soft purple is a close relation. In this small galley kitchen it creates a more consistent impression.**
Above **The unifomity in color means more emphasis can be placed on details such as door and drawers handles, display, and storage.**

If the kitchen cabinets are natural wood most colors will be suitable, either in a similar tone or in direct contrast. If the units are already painted, lacquered, or stained, then the color chosen for the rest of the room should be selected with the cabinet color in mind, since they tend to be a dominant feature in a kitchen.

For example, if you opt for a bright blue finish to the cabinets, a subtle burnt-orange wash on the walls or a paler turquoise-blue matte-finish paint can make the scheme modern and vibrant. The same cabinets set against plain white walls may give it a Mediterranean feel that could be accentuated with accessories such as simple hand-painted ceramics and plain terra-cotta plates and bowls. The same cabinets again, but this

time with yellow walls and simple blue-, white-, and yellow-striped soft furnishing could hint at the colors found at the Impressionist artist Claude Monet's house in France.

Lack of color can also be an interesting feature. If you have a plain white kitchen with pale wood or steel fittings the accessories you add will be features. The lack of color will also make it appear timeless, and if the walls are simply white they will be easily touched up or repainted when the surfaces begin to look a little worn or damaged.

Black is an interesting color, but one that many people avoid in kitchens. Black can make a room seem small and stuffy, but used in carefully controlled amounts it can be very dramatic. For example, an item

in the kitchen that is a necessity but not necessarily an asset to the room, like a radiator, could be cased in and painted black so that it becomes featureless. Kickboards under units will seem to disappear if painted black, and matte black walls can double as giant chalkboards on which shopping lists, poems, and phone numbers can be scribbled.

Black detailing can be used to accentuate the shape and design of a piece of furniture or an architectural feature in the room. This emphasis can be done within the edge of a door panel or at the edge of a drawer or cupboard to create the impression of a frame. Black on natural wood is very effective, but the same result can be achieved with other dark contrasting colors, such as navy or gray.

flooring

Opposite **A simple checkerboard pattern is traditional in black and white, but it can be brought up to date by using different colors.**
Left **On either side of this cabinet and sink insets of red brick paving stones are set in a block pattern, which contrasts with the borders, façades, surfaces, and steps, which are white marble.**
Below **This striped effect is achieved with three tones of laminate floor covering that contrast with the solid color of the cabinets.**

The priorities for a kitchen floor covering are that it should be a safe, nonslip surface and easy to clean. There are many types of flooring to choose from, but remember that the finished floor will only be as good as the surface beneath it. Make sure that the base onto which the floor will be laid is clean, even, and well prepared, otherwise the faults will be magnified when the flooring is laid.

Tile and stone

Floor tiles must not to be confused with those intended for work surface use. They are thicker and larger, and are made to withstand the wear and tear of being underfoot. There are two categories: natural and decorative. Natural tiles are made with different types of baked clay—terra-cotta tiles are the most common. Their color depends on the clay used: it can vary from rich red to creamier tones. Quarry tiles, made from durable unrefined aluminum clay, are fired at high temperatures and less porous than many other types of clay tile. Prices for these tiles vary. Handmade tiles are the most expensive, but some manufacturers mechanically produce tiles with a slightly irregular look that will create the same overall effect less expensively.

Although not technically a tile, bricks are made of clay and fired, so may be included in this section. Bricks come in a range of colors, from creamy brown to traditional red and those with blue and purple hues. This comparatively cheap and hardwearing material can be laid in herringbone and other patterns or in simple rows.

Decorative tiles are generally glazed ceramic shapes, usually square, but sometimes oblong or hexagonal. These tiles can have a high sheen or a matte finish and come in a rainbow assortment of colors and patterns. They are easy to clean, but may be slippery underfoot if a spill occurs. Ceramic tiles may also break if a heavy object is dropped on them; the broken or cracked tile can be replaced but it is a difficult job to remove a single tile when it is grouted. Ceramic tiles offer infinite opportunities to create patterns and mix colors, from simple checkerboards to complex designs.

Marble, granite, slate, limestone, Yorkstone, and sandstone are all in the category of stone. The slabs or tiles are larger than the average ceramic tile and because they are heavy they are best used

Above **Following the rise of interest in the New Professional kitchen and restaurant-style ranges and large refrigerators, many other industrial products, such as flooring, have found their way from the commercial world into the home environment. This raised rubber floor covering, originally designed for use in hospitals and warehouses, is sturdy and durable and the raised circles make it slip resistant. Many companies are now extending their color ranges to cater to the requirements of the home market.**

Top right **Heavy-duty textured glass bricks, which are often used in sidewalks or outside walls to bring light into basements, have been used here to create a small matlike inset into the tiled floor. They make an unusual and stylish but practical and easy-to-maintain floor covering.**

Right **Textured linoleum is practical, easy to clean, and warm underfoot.**

Opposite **This floor is covered in a staggered pattern of Italian tiles, which are cool and hard, but waterproof and simple to mop clean.**

on ground-level floors. These rigid and often uneven stones can be difficult to lay, so it is a job best done by a professional. A stone floor is hard-wearing and will withstand any amount of wear, tear, and water. The disadvantages are that it is cold under foot (though this can be counteracted by underfloor heating) and hard (china and glass dropped on a stone floor will invariably break, whereas on softer surfaces there is a chance they would survive intact).

Marble comes in a wide range of colors and types, from the classic white Italian with gray veins to rich reds and greens, such as Irish Connemara varieties. Marble can be expensive if you buy solid tiles, but if you opt for a thin veneer of marble laid on a cement or concrete base you can keep the cost down. It is solid and easy to maintain, but a marble floor may become slippery when wet.

Sheet and soft flooring

Linoleum is made from linseed oil, finely ground wood flour, and pine resin, with a jute backing. Fashionable in the 1940s and '50s, in recent years it has seen a steady revival. Often referred to as "lino," it comes in rolls and in easier-to-manage tiles. It is easy to brush and mop clean, and a polish or finish can be applied if required.

Vinyl is lino's brighter and more versatile younger sister. It is a chemical-based product, with an infinite range of colors and patterns. It is

Above and right **Two different types of flooring have been used here—wood and slate—and the zigzag edge where the two floors meet echos the irregular join of the plaster ceiling and glass extension. By using two different types of flooring definition can be given to different areas in the same room: wood in the kitchen and slate in the dining/seating area.**
Opposite **Wood is an attractive and warm floor covering but it should be well sealed and finished to prevent water and wear damage. Wooden planks and parquet can be laid in many ways to form patterns and optical effects that can make a room appear longer or wider.**

hardwearing and long lasting, but for all its good qualities it is worth noting that the surface will be affected by burns and grit, which will mark the top layer. Some types of vinyl flooring have to be sealed with a recommended finish, but this need be applied only two or three times a year, even in a busy traffic area. Cushioned vinyl has a soft, slightly spongy backing. Sometimes patterns are stamped into the two layers, giving the motif a three-dimensional appearance. If heavy furniture rests on this type of floor it will dent the surface, so to avoid permanent damage put protective cups or shields over the leg ends.

Rubber usually comes from industrial sources and should be laid on a concrete or similarly smooth, solid base. Available in a range of colors and raised relief patterns, rubber floors are very good in a contemporary setting.

Cork's warm, soft surface has made it a popular floor covering for many years, and as there are both floor- and wall- quality cork tiles it is best to check that you are getting the right type. Tiles are usually impregnated with a polyurethane seal to make them more resistant to water; check they are sealed before you lay them. Although the natural golden honey color of plain cork tiles has been perennially popular, manufacturers now supply cork in a range of colors that can be used to create different patterns and effects.

Coir or sisal matting, made from natural fibers such as coconut husk and agave leaves, is hardwearing and, if pretreated, can be stain resistant, but it should not be used near a sink or stove where it can come into contact with excess water, a spark, or fat. Make sure you have an effective vacuum cleaner, as food trapped in this type of matting can be difficult to remove and may, in extreme cases, decay and lead to ant or other inset infestation.

Wood

Wood makes an attractive and timeless flooring. There are so many different varieties and colors of wood, as well as ways of laying it, that there is a type of wooden floor to suit every style of kitchen design and every taste, whether you opt for long plain boards laid in parallel lines, parquet with its tighter geometric design, or more ornate patterns such as herringbone laid in an interconnecting "V" construction. The versatility of wood goes beyond the designs that can be achieved in its laying; it also has wide color prospects too. It can be left natural, enhanced with just a little wax or clear varnish, stained to a richer, darker hue, painted in bright primary colors with decorative borders, or given a pale, subtle overall colorwash.

There are two main families of wood—hard and soft. Hardwoods, such as elm, walnut, ash, oak, and maple tend, to be in the upper price bracket and in some cases are rare or difficult to procure because they are environmentally protected species, and they should only be bought if they can be accredited as coming from managed forests. Softwoods, such as pine, are invariably from managed woods. These trees take less time to grow and are a easily renewable source. Pine is cheaper than hardwoods and more economical to use if you are going to paint or stain the floor. You can use basic latex or marine paint, which is very durable, but it takes a long time to dry and comes in a limited range of colors. All wood floors in a kitchen environment, whether natural, stained, or painted, must be sealed. There are various types of sealant, from wax polish, matte and polyurethane varnish, to high-gloss deck varnish, but it is important to choose the right type of finish to suit the rest of your decor.

sources

Many of these companies are manufacturers and sell their products nationally through local distributors. Call for a catalog and/or a list of dealers near you.

Kitchen Cabinets and Design

There is a great deal of overlap in the kitchen industry. Some companies design and install only complete kitchens, some offer freestanding cabinetry, most offer both. If an entry is marked (C), the company does only custom work. Nearly all of the companies listed are members of the National Kitchen and Bath Association. For information on NKBA members in your area, call 800-401-KNBA or 800-367-6522.

American Woodmark Corp.
3120 Shawnee Drive
Winchester, VA 22601
800-388-2483
www.american
woodmark.com
Manufactures cabinets and accessories, such as slide-out wastebaskets, pull-down cookbook rack, and pull-out shelves, in various woods

BathClick.com
121 Fieldcrest Avenue
Edison, NJ 08837
800-643-9990
www.bathclick.com
Largest collection of luxury sinks, faucets, cabinets, and accessories anywhere.

Becker Zeyko
1030 Marina Village Parkway
Alameda, CA 94501
510-865-1616
www.beckerzeyko.com
This high-end cabinetry is manufactured with the highest environmentally conscious standards using earth-friendly materials and bio-degradable products.

BentWood Custom Kitchens (C)
4508 Lovers Lane
Dallas, TX 75205
214-750-0271
www.bentwoodkitchens.com
Custom cabinets from high tech to Old World. Custom finishes matched to fabric and wallpaper.

Colonial Craft Kitchens (C)
344 West Main Street
Annville, PA 17003
717-867-1145
www.colonialkitchens.com
High-end custom cabinet making. Unique painted and stained wood finishes. Artistic approach emphasized.

Christians (C)
212-333-8794
Now widely available in the U.S., this British manufacturer offers the best in fitted furniture for the kitchen in five classic styles.

Holiday Kitchens (C)
A division of Mastercraft Industries, Inc.
120 West Allen Street
Rice Lake, WI 54868
715-234-8111
www.holidaykitchens.com
Fine custom kitchens at excellent prices have kept this company in business for over 50 years. Cabinets are shipped all over the country.

Ikea
U.S. Flagship location:
1800 East Mc Connor, Parkway
Schaumburg, IL 60173
mail order and online store:
www.ikea.com
Home basics at great prices, including assembly kit furniture and stylish, inexpensive kitchenware.

Irpinia Kitchens (C)
7600 North Federal Highway, Suite 103
Boca Raton, FL 33487
561-988-0990
www.irpinia.com
A mix of exotic woods and bright paints set kitchens from this Canadian manufacturer apart from the rest. Everything is finished with a high-gloss polyester finish for a mirrorlike effect.

Kitchen Center
1105 Burke Street
Winston Salem, NC 29101
336-725-2343
www.thekitchencenter.com
Features all top-rated kitchen products such as Wood-Mode cabinets, DuPont Corian countertops, Hansa faucets, Viking and Thermador ovens and ranges, and Sub-Zero refrigerators.

KraftMaid Cabinetry, Inc.
16052 Industrial Parkway
Middlefield, OH 44062
888-562-7744
www.kraftmaid.com
Quality construction is the hallmark of this company's affordable cabinetry, available in a range of styles, from traditional to contemporary.

Poggenpohl U.S., Inc.
150 East 58th Street
New York, NY 10022
800-987-0553
www.poggenpohl-usa.com
Clean, modern lines are the signature of this 100+-year-old European kitchen design firm. They offer more than 180 front styles in wood, lacquer, and laminates.

Merillat
5353 West U.S. 223
Adrian, MI 49221
800-845-7314
www.merillat.com
Makers of standard particleboard cabinets with a wide variety of wood

veneer fronts, this company is best known for its "frameless" construction.

Quaker Maid Kitchens
1880 Central Park Ave.
Yonkers, NY 10710
914-979-1000
www.quakermaid.com
Specializes in combining standard components with care for custom-look kitchens.

Rutt Custom Cabinetry (C)
P.O. Box 129
1564 Main Street
Goodville, PA 17528
800-220-RUTT
www.rutt1.com
This fine cabinetmaker can reproduce the characteristics of any number of eras and styles, built to your specifications.

Sears, Roebuck and Company
800-MY-SEARS
www.sears.com
Working with local contractors, Sears resurfaces cabinets and drawers to change the look of a kitchen with little fuss and at minimum cost.

SieMatic Corporation
Two Greenwood Square
3331 Street Road,
Suite 450, PA 19020
215-244-6800
www.siematic.com
This system of modular cabinets offers ultimate flexibility, fine craftsmanship, and style.

Starmark Cabinets, Inc. (C)
A division of Custom Made Co.
600 East 48th Street,
North Sioux Falls, SD 57104
800-594-9444
www.starmarkcabinetry.com
Specializes in fine cabinetry with a variety of fronts and surfaces at competitive prices.

Wellborn Cabinet, Inc.
P.O. Box 1210
Ashland, AL 36251
800-336 8040 ext.216
www.wellborncabinet.com
Offers stock wooden cabinets in many different sizes with many different fronts, giving thousands of options for a seemingly custom-designed kitchen.

Wm Ohs (C)
115 Madison
Denver, CO 80206
303-321-3232
www.wmohs.com
These elegant, traditional kitchens are custom built in America and are available in all periods and varieties of decorating styles.

Wood-Mode Custom Cabinetry
800-635-7500
www.wood-mode.com
This extensive line features many door styles, finishes, and special-purpose built-in features.

Flooring

(See also Ceramic Tiles and Backsplashes)

Armstrong
P.O. Box 3001
Lancaster, PA 17604
800-233-3823
www.armstrong.com
Makers of sheet vinyl and vinyl tile in a wide variety of colors, finishes, and styles.

Banta Tile & Marble
1284 Loop Road
Lancaster, PA 17601
717-393-3931
www.bantatile.com
This custom fabricator of stone produces backsplashes, counters, and floors. Decorative tiles to coordinate are available.

Bruce Hardwood Floors
16803 Dallas Parkway
Addison, TX 75248
800-722-4647
www.brucehardwoodfloors.com
Features style options and hardwood patterns to create a variety of different looks. Special finishes are available to protect from scratching, scuffing, and wear.

Congoleum
P.O. Box 3127
3705 Quakerbridge Road
Mercerville, NJ 08619
800-934-3567
www.congoleum.com
This service-oriented company manufactures a complete line of sheet vinyls, vinyl tiles, and wood laminates in an extraordinary variety of colors and patterns.

Kahrs International
1558 B Street, #101
Hayward, CA 94541
800-800-5247
www.kahrs.com
A special acrylic finish and unique construction make these widely distributed wood floors perfect for high-traffic areas such as a kitchen.

Mannington Resilient Floors
A division of Mannington Mills, Inc.
75 Mannington Road
Salem, NJ 08079
800-356-6787
www.mannington.com
Manufacturers of sheet vinyl, composition tiles, inlaid vinyl, and wood laminates in designs. patterns, and colors ranging from traditional to high fashion.

Pergo Original® Flooring
800-337-3746
www.pergo.com
Distributors of high-pressure melamine laminate from Sweden, guaranteed for 15 years not to wear, fade, or stain.

Tarkett Flooring, Inc.
1139 Leheigh Avenue
Whitehall, PA 18052
800-367-8275
A pioneer in color, design, and technology of long-lasting sheet vinyl floors.

Wilsonart® Flooring
P.O. Box 6110
2400 Wilson Place
Temple, TX 76503-6110
800-433-3222
www.wilsonart.com
Durability and design flexibility combine in this new laminate flooring, available in wood grain, marble, and stone looks. Wilsonart also manufacturers a wide variety of countertop surfaces, both laminate (e.g., Formica®) and solid (e.g., Corian®).

Ceramic Tiles and Backsplashes

Ann Sacks Tile & Stone
1210 SE Grand Avenue
Portland, OR 97214
503 233-0611
www.annsacks.com
Limestone, terra-cotta, marble mosaics, handcrafted and handpainted tile, stone antiquities.

Country Floors, Inc.
8735 Melrose Avenue
Los Angeles, CA 90069
310-657-0510
Handcrafted, decorative, contemporary art tiles; terra-cotta floors and moldings; antiqued and tumbled marble; limestone and travertine; mosaics; sturdy floor tiles. Imported tiles are regularly stocked in New York and Los Angeles stores. American tiles are made to order.

Florida Tile Industries
P.O. Box 447
Lakeland, FL 33802
800-789-TILE
This company offers a wide variety of the latest in floor, wall, and accent tiles from many manufacturers worldwide.

Wholesale Tile & Accessories
1902 Flagler Street
Tampa, FL 33605
813-248-0455
Importers of handmade tiles from Europe and South America.

Countertops and Work Islands

Dal-Tile/American Olean Tile Co.
7834 Hawn Freeway
Dallas, TX 75217
800-933-8453
The merger of these pre-eminent tile companies has created the largest and most complete tile distributor in the country.

DuPont Corian®
Barley Mill Plaza
Price Mill Building
P.O. Box 80012
Wilmington, DE 19880-0012
800-426-7426
www.dupont.com/corian/
This nonporous acrylic surface is used for countertops and sinks. Patterns and colors are consistent throughout the piece. Stains or scratches can easily be ground out.

Formica®
10155 Reading Road
Cincinnati, OH 45241
800-367-6422
www.formica.com
This well-known laminate can mimic nearly any matte, shiny, or pattern-textured surface you can think of.

Get Real Surfaces
3 Buckingham Avenue
Poughkeepsie, NY 12601
345-452-3988
This custom manufacturer of concrete products in any color, including countertops, sinks, floor and wall tiles, suggests you fax a drawing for a quote on your project.

Wilsonart®
See under Flooring

Sinks, Faucets, Hardware, and Accessories

The Antique Hardware and Home Store
19 Buckingham
Plantation Drive
Bluffton, SC 29910
800-422-9982
www.antiquehardware.com
Creators of reproductions of vintage sinks and faucets. Call for their catalog.

Blanco
1050 Taylors Lane
Unit 4
Cinnaminson, NJ 08077
800-451-5782
www.blanco-america.com
Dependable source for sinks and accessories, including a home waste recycling center.

Delta
P.O. Box 40980
55 East 111th Street
Indianapolis, IN 46280
800-345-3358
www.deltafaucet.com
Well known for their brass faucets manufactured with noncompression construction, superbly completed with a tarnish-resistant Brilliance™ finish.

Elkay
2222 Camden Court
Oak Brook, IL 60523
630-574-8484
www.elkay.com
Their sinks individualize your kitchen by featuring different shapes, compartments, and finishes.

Franke, Inc.
Kitchen Systems Division
3050 Campus Drive,
Suite 500
Hatfield, PA 19440
800-626-5771
www.frankeksd.com
International manufacturer of highest quality stainless-steel, granite, and titanium sink systems, faucets, custom accessories, water filters, and dispensing units.

Hansgrohe, Inc.
1465 Ventura Drive
Cumming, GA 30040
800-719-1000
www.hansgrohe.com
Ergonomic European styling, quality materials, and state-of-the-art engineering are the hallmarks of this faucet company.

Just Manufacturing
9233 King Street
Franklin Park, IL 60131
847-678-5150
www.justsinks.com
This company produces over 500 models of top-of-the-line stainless-steel sinks. All are nonporous and sound deadened.

Kindred
1000 Kindred Road
Midland, Ontario
Canada, L4R 4K9
888-530-7406
www.kindred-sinkware.com
Manufacturers of more than 100 configurations of the finest quality stainless-steel sinks. European styling and a unique overflow feature make them very desirable.

Kohler Company
444 Highland Drive
Kohler, WI 53044
800-4-KOHLER
(456-4537)
www.kohlerco.com
A full range of kitchen and entertainment sinks in colored baked enamels and metals, as well as faucets and decorative accessories.

Moen, Inc.
Al Moen Drive
North Olmsted, OH 44070-8022
800-553-6636
www.moen.com
Moen produces a full line of faucets, most of which are single handle. They are of fine quality, easy to maintain, and all come with a lifetime guarantee.

Price Pfister
13500 Paxton street
Pacoima, CA
800-732-8238
www.pricepfister.com
Producers of high-caliber kitchen faucets with elegant styling and a lifetime warrantee covering both finish and function for as long as you own your home.

Rapetti Faucets
Zero High Street
Plainville, MA 02762
800-688-5500
These moderately priced high-end faucets are manufactured in Italy. Their acclaimed designs and finishes have won them many competitions.

Sterling Plumbing
2900 Golf Road
Rolling Meadows,
IL 60008
800-783-7546
www.sterlingplumbing.com
Known for their stainless-steel and fiberglass-sheet-molded composite sinks designed to be quiet and kind to china and glasswear. Matching faucets are part of the line.

Built-in and Major Appliances

AGA Ranges
6400 Highlands Parkway
Smyrna, GA 30082
800-633-9200
This custom-assembled cooker can broil, roast, bake, simmer, fry, steam, stew, toast, boil, and clean itself.

Amana Appliances
2800 220th Trail
Box 8901
Amana, IA 52204
800-843-0304
Manufacturers all major kitchen appliances, highly regarded for their top quality and high energy-efficient ratings.

Asko Dishwashers and Washer-Dryers
P.O. Box 851805
Richardson,
TX 75085-1805
972-644-8595
Ecologically minded makers of dishwashers that have stainless steel interiors, superior quietness, and produce sparkling results without prerinsing. Their washers save 15,000 gallons of water annually, while getting clothes cleaner.

Dacor Epicure Appliances
950 South Raymond Avenue
Pasadena, CA 91109
626-799-1000
Offer commercial-style cooktops, ranges, ovens, and hoods with superior performance, many features, and benefits.

Dynasty
A division of
Jade Range, Inc.
7355 East Slauson Avenue
Commerce, CA 90040
888-4MAYTAG
www.dynastyrange.com
Produces a versatile oven that can operate in conventional or convection mode, bake, broil, and defrost. It includes a built-in top grill.

Frigidaire
P.O. Box 7181
Dublin, OH 43017-0781
800-374-4432
www.frigidaire.com
Perhaps best known for their refrigerators and freezers, this company makes a complete line of kitchen appliances, right down to disposals and built-in microwave ovens.

GE Appliance Headquarters
AP6 Room 129
Louisville, KY 40225
800-626-2000
www.geappliances.com
From water softening systems, disposals, and compactors to the more usual kitchen appliances, GE has it all, in both gas and electric.

Gaggenau USA Corporation
425 University Avenue
Norwood, MA 02062
800-929-1125
www.gaggenau.com
These custom-designed built-in cooktops, ovens, ventilator hoods, and electric grills have a sleek European look featuring stainless-steel finishes.

Jenn-Air
240 Edwards Street SE
Cleveland, TN 37311
800-688-1100
www.jennair.com
This company is a leader in both freestanding and built-in stoves, convection ovens, and vented indoor grills.

KitchenAid
P.O. Box 218
St. Joseph, MI 49085
800-422-1230
www.kitchenaid.com
While best known for their dishwashers, KitchenAid makes all appliances necessary for a complete kitchen, including countertop appliances such as mixers, toasters, and blenders.

Magic Chef Co.
240 Edwards Street SE
Cleveland, TN 37311
800-688-1120
When looking for a basic gas or electric stove or microwave, this company can fill the bill.

Maytag Customer Service
240 Edwards Street SE
Cleveland, TN 37311
800-688-9900
www.maytag.com
Known for dependability, and most famous for their washers and dryers, this company makes a full line of kitchen appliances, large and small.

Miele
220 Worlds Fair Drive
Somerset, NJ 08873
609-419-9898
www.mieleusa.com
This European company is best know in the U.S. for its attention to detail in high-end dishwashers, ovens, and vacuum cleaners.

Northland
P.O. Box 400
Greenville, MI 48838-0400
800-223-3900
www.northlandnka.com
Will customize refrigerators and freezers in virtually any size desired. The doors are customized with panels of the same wood used elsewhere in the kitchen.

Signature Marketing/ Garland Residential Products
513 Belmont Avenue
Helidon, NJ 07508
800-358-8886
www.garland-group.com
Garland/U.S. Range sells insulated residential versions of its top-of-the-line commercial ranges for the serious home cook.

Sub-Zero
P.O. Box 4130
Madison, WI 57344-4130
800-222-7820
www.subzero.com
Custom makers of refrigerators, refrigerated drawers, freezers, and ice maker drawers that can be had with brushed stainless-steel fronts or fronts can be added by consumer to match cabinetry.

Thermador
5551 McFadden
Huntington Beach, CA 92649
800-656-9226
www.thermador.com
Their cooktops and stoves have an ExtraLow® burner system that cycles on and off, allowing you to simmer foods at exceptionally low temperatures without fear of burning.

Viking Range
111 Front Street
Greenwood, MS 38930
888-845-4641
www.vikingrange.com
Known for professional-quality cooking, ventilation, and cleanup equipment designed for the home kitchen,including innovative warming drawers.

Whirlpool
800-253-1301
www.whirlpool.com
Well-known company offering a full line gas and electric appliances, designed with ease of use and time saving in mind. Small apartment- and college-size refrigerators are a specialty.

Wolf Range Co.
19600 South Alameda Street
Compton, CA 90221
310-637-3737
www.wolfrange.com
Supplies commercial ranges from 500 to 600 BTUs that have been insulated and are approved for home use.

Exhaust Hoods and Exhaust Fans

Broan
926 West State Street
Hartford, WI 53027
800-558-1711
www.broan.com
This company offers a wide variety of duct and ductless hoods in a number of enamel colors and stainless steel.

Modern-Aire Ventilating
7319 Lankershim Boulevard
North Hollywood, CA 91605
818-765-9870
www.modernaire.com
Makers of standard and custom-designed stainless-steel range hoods. Stainless-steel panels can also be designed to fit fronts of other kitchen appliances for a coordinated look.

Vent-A-Hood
1000 North Greenville
Richardson, TX 75083
972-235-5201
www.ventahood.com
This 65-year-old company was the first to create ventilation systems for residential use. Their unique system uses centrifugal force rather than filters to remove grease from the air.

Lighting

Juno Lighting
1300 South Wolf Road
Des Plaines, IL 60018
800-323-5068
www.junolighting.com
Manufacturers of sleek, modern track and recessed lighting for custom installations.

Hafele America Company
3901 Cheyenne Drive
P.O.Box 4000
Archdale, NC 27263
800-334-1873
336-889-2322
www.hafeleonline.com
Look to this task lighting company for under-cabinet lighting. Systems are available in florescent and halogen, and may be built in or added on.

Kichler Lighting Group
7711 East Pleasant Valley Road
Cleveland, OH 44131
800-659-9000
216-573-1000
www.kichler.com
This manufacturer can provide any type of lighting in any style, from chandeliers to under-counter florescents and everything in between.

Electrics Lighting and Design
530 West Francisco, Suite H
San Rafeal, CA 94901
415-258-9996
This firm distributes over 100 different lighting lines, most from Italy with additions from Spain and America and emphasis on modern looks.

Lightolier (task lighting)
631 Airport Road
Fall River, MA 02720
800-217-7722
www.lightolier.com
Whether under-counter, pin spot, surface mounted, or general, this company supplies all types of kitchen lighting in a contemporary vein.

NuLite Ltd.
7001 East 57th Place
Commerce City, CO
303-287-9646
www.nulite.net
Best known for florescent fixtures, this company provides many different types and styles of kitchen lighting.

Progress Lighting
P.O. Box 5704
Spartenburg, SC 29304
864-599-6000
www.progresslighting.com
Suppliers of all types of kitchen lighting, including toe space lighting for delightful night lights. Much of their work is done through builders.

Sea Gull Lighting
P.O. Box 329
Riverside, NJ 08075
856-764-0500
www.seagulllighting.com
This company offers lighting fixtures in a broad range of styles.

W.A.C. Lighting
113-25 14th Avenue
College Point, NY 11356
800-526-2588
www.waclighting.com
This manufacturer is known for its discreet and subtle track and recessed lighting to be used where light is wanted but not obvious fixtures.

Countertop Appliances and Accessories

Anaheim Manufacturing Co.
4240 East La Palma Avenue
Anaheim, CA 92807
800-669-8925
www.anaheimmfg.com
Produces a high-quality garbage disposal unit (Waste King) that runs at a higher RPM than most, making it less likely to jam and easier to unjam. Another well-known product is their hot water dispenser.

Black & Decker
6 Armstrong Road
Shelton, CT 06484
800-231-9786
www.blackanddecker.com
If it's a small kitchen appliance, B & D makes it. Their quality is excellent and their low-key designs blend in without being easily dated. A new premium line, kitchenTools™ incorporates industrial design elements.

Everpure, Inc.
660 Blackhawk Drive
Westmont, IL 60559
800-323-7873
www.everpure.com
This company produces a drinking water purifying system for the home that installs under the sink using a separate faucet. It can also be attached to water systems in refrigerators.

In-Sink-Erator
4700 21st Street
Racine, WI 53406
800-558-5700
www.insinkerator.com
This company is known for their low-maintenance disposals and hot water systems.

Kinetico
10845 Kinsman Road
Newbury, OH 44065
800-944-9283
www.kinetico.com
Install this manufacturer's reverse osmosis filtering system unit to the water line in the basement or under the sink and add a dedicated faucet to enjoy pure water.

Kitchen Sink Antiques
North Carolina, 27613
www.kitchensinkantiques.com
Specializes in all periods of glassware, dinnerware, kitchenware, restaurant china, and pottery.

Once Upon a Table
30 Crofut Street
Pittsfield, MA 01201
413-443-6622
www.onceuponatable.com
A wonderful collection of European and American period kitchenware; jadelite, bakelite, FireKing, biscuit bins, and much more.

Sharp Electronics Corp.
Sharp Plaza
Mahwah, NJ 07430
800-237-4277
www.sharp-usa.com
The first and, many think still the best, in the microwave area. Controls are kept simple with no more information than you need. The latest trick is recipes on the keypad.

U-Line
8900 North 55th Street
Milwaukee, WI 53223
414-354-0300
This company excels in the construction of built-in ice makers, wine coolers, under-counter refrigerators.

Companies and individuals whose work is featured in this book (numbers following addresses refer to the pages on which their work is featured).

Architects and Designers

Ash Sakula Architects
Studio 115
38 Mount Pleasant
London WC1X 0AN
England
+44 (0)20-7837- 9735

20–22, 26–27, 44–47, 68–69, 161 below right, 172 right, 173 180

Rick Baker
F2 Cross Lane
London N8 7SA
England
+44 (0)20-8340-2020

108–9, 114 below right, 164, 172 left

Bruce Bierman Design Inc.
29 West 15th Street
New York, NY 10011
212-243-1935

18–19

Laura Bohn Design Associates
30 West 26th Street
New York, NY 10010
212-645-3636

60–63

Felix Bonnier
7 rue St. Claude
Paris 75003
France
+33 (0)1-42-26-09-83

95, 110, 123

Mark Brook Design
7 Sunderland Terrace
London W2 5PA
England
+44 (0)20-7221-8106

86–87, 100 below, 140 above & below right, 179

Carnachan Architects Ltd
27 Bath Street, Parnell
P.O. Box 37–717
Auckland
New Zealand

64–65

Circus Architects
1a Summers Street
London EC1R 5BD
England
+44 (0)20-7833-1999

12, 103 above, 124, 148–49 155 above

Halstead Designs International
9 Warwick Square
London SW1V 2AA
England
+44 (0)20 7834 2511
and **Halstead Designs New York Inc.,**
515 East 72nd Street # 14L
New York, NY 10021
212-879-1090

111 below right, 158 above right

Hester Gray
25 Pembridge Villas
London W11 3EP
England
+44 (0)20-7229-3162

82–85, 140 below left & below center, 155 below

Amanda Hannam W.H. Designs
27 Gloucester Street
London SW1V 2DB
England
+44 (0)20-7834-4424

111 center & center right, 137 above right

Jack Ingram Bookworks
34 Ansleigh Place
London W11 4BW
England
+44 (0)20-7792-8310

88–89, 98, 117 below, 179

INTERIORS Geneva
15 rue Verdaine
Geneva 1204
Switzerland
+41 (0)22-310-41-35
and **INTERIORS bis**
60 Sloane Avenue
London SW3 3DD
England
+44 (0)20-7838-1104

50–1

Interni Interior Design Consultancy
15–19 Boundary Street
Rushcutters Bay
Sydney 2011
New South Wales
Australia

103 below, 154 below left, 159

IPL Interiors
Unit 28C1 Thames House
140 Battersea Park Road
London SW11 4NY
England
+44 (0)20-7622-3009

99 below left, 128 above left

Larcombe & Solomon Architects
Level 3
397 Riley Street
Surry Hills
Sydney 2010
New South Wales
Australia

104

Kayode Lipede
+44 (0)20-7794-7535

103 above, 148–49

John Mainwaring & Associates Pty Ltd
P.O. Box 958
Noosa Heads
Queensland 4567
Australia
+61 (0)7-5449-0622

100 above

Marino & Giolito
161 West 16th Street
New York, NY 10011
212-260-8142

139 above & center right, 157 above, 178 below

Marshall Haines and Barrow
35 Alfred Place
London WC1E 7DP
England

40–43

Jean-Louis Ménard
32 Boulevard de l'Hopital
Paris 75005
France
+33 (0)1-43-36-31-74

52–55, 139 center

Charles Morris Mount
300 West 108th Street #2C
New York, NY 10025
212-864-2937

122 above left, 154 center left, 177 right

Andrew Parr
SJB Interior Design
P O Box 1149
South Melbourne 3205
Australia
+61 (0)3-9688-2122

6–7

Peter Romaniuk
The Flower House
Cynthia Street
London N1 9JF
England
+44 (0)20-7837-7373

78–81, 101, 113 below, 141

Luigi Rosellli
Surry Hills, Sydney 2010
New South Wales
Australia
+61 (0)2-9281-1498

177 left

Sophie Sarin
+44 (0)20-7221 4635

70–71, 174–75

Schack-Arnott
Danish Classic Moderne
517 High Street
Prahan, Victoria 3181
Australia
+61 (0)3-9525-0250

150 below

Tony Suttle
Woods Baget Pty Ltd
64 Marine Parade
Southport, Queensland 4000
Australia

170

Stephen Varady Architecture
Studio 5
102 Albion Street
Surry Hills
Sydney 2010 , New South Wales
Australia
+61 (0)2-9281-4825

126, 133, 150 above, 171 above right

Hervé Vermesch
50 rue Bichat
Paris 75010
France
+33 (0)1-42-01-39-39

106, 124–25, 143, 152 below 181 below

Consuelo Zoelly
5–7 rue Mont Louis
Paris 75011
France
+33 (0)1-42-62-19-95

97, 107, 119, 152–53

Kitchen Companies

Bulthaup UK Ltd
37 Wigmore Street
London W1H 9LD
England
+44 (0)20-7495-3663

2

Chalon
The Plaza
535 Kings Road
London SW10 0SZ
England
+44 (0)20-7351-0008

36–37, 40–43, 111 above right

Crabtree Kitchens
The Twickenham Center
Norcutt Road
Twickenham TW2 6SR
England
+44 (0)20-8755-1121

66–67, 144 below

Rhode Design
86 Stoke Newington Church Street
London N16 0AP
England
+44 (0)20-7275-8261

131 center right, 144 above, 145

Smallbone of Devizes
The Hopton Workshop
Devizes
Wiltshire SN10 2EU
England
+44 (0)20-7589-5998

146–47

Acknowledgments

The publisher thanks the following individuals and organizations for their kind permission to reproduce the photographs in this book:

1 an apartment in Paris designed by Hervé Vermesch; **2–3** Melvyn Gadsdon's loft in London/kitchen by Bulthaup; **4–5** Sussie Ahlburg and Andy Keate's house in London; **6–7** Andrew Parr's house in Melbourne; **8–9** Sally Butler's house in London; **12** Victor Ktori's loft in London designed by Circus Architects; **14–17** Sussie Ahlburg and Andy Keate's house in London; **18–19** Bruce Bierman's loft in New York; **20–22** a house in London designed by Ash Sakula Architects; **23** Polly Dickens and Mark Gilbey's loft in London; **26–27** a house in London designed by Ash Sakula Architects; **28–29** Baron and Baroness de Mitri de Gunzburg's house in Provence; **30** Sussie Ahlburg and Andy Keate's house in London; **31** Marilyn Phipps' house in Kent; **32–33** Polly Dickens and Mark Gilbey's loft in London; **34** Sussie Ahlburg and Andy Keate's house in London; **35** *above* Sussie Ahlburg and Andy Keate's house in London; **35** *below* Douglas and Dorothy Hamilton's apartment in New York; **36–37** kitchen by Chalon; **38** Suzanne Slesin and Michael Steinberg's apartment in New York designed by architect Jean-Louis Ménard; **40–43** Mr. and Mrs. Barrow's house in Surrey designed by architects Marshall, Haines, and Barrow/kitchen by Chalon; **44–47** Ash Sakula's house in London; **48–49** Janick and Hubert Schoumacher-Vilfroy's house in Normandy; **50–51** a house in the Luberon designed by Françoise de Pfyffer/INTERIORS Geneva and INTERIORS bis London; **52–55** Suzanne Slesin and Michael Steinberg's apartment in New York designed by architect Jean-Louis Ménard/cabinetry and doors by John Marshall Contracting; **58–59** Etienne and Mary Millner's house in London; **60–63** a house in Pennsylvania designed by Laura Bohn and built by Richard Fiore/BFI Construction; **64–65** Robyn and Simon Carnachan's house in Auckland; **66–67** Nigel Rowe's house in Middlesex/kitchen by Crabtree Kitchens; **68–69** an apartment in London designed by Ash Sakula Architects; **70–71** Sophie Sarin's apartment in London; **72–73** John Alexander and Fiona Waterstreet's loft in New York designed by Lorraine Kirke; **74–77** Jan Staller's loft in New York, ; **78–81** Paula Pryke and Peter Romaniuk's house in London; **82–85** Rose Gray's apartment in London designed by Hester Gray; **86–87** Stephen Woodham's house in London designed in conjunction with Mark Brook Design; **88–89** Christine Walsh and Ian Bartlett's house in London designed by Jack Ingham of Bookworks; **94** an apartment in New York designed by Marino & Giolito; **95** Felix Bonnier's apartment in Paris; **96** *left* John Alexander and Fiona Waterstreet's loft in New York designed by Lorraine Kirke; **97** Consuelo Zoelly's apartment in Paris; **98** Christine Walsh and Ian Bartlett's house in London designed by Jack Ingham of Bookworks; **99** *center left* an apartment in London designed by Ash Sakula Architects; **99** *below left* a house in London designed by François Gilles and Dominique Lubar of IPL Interiors; **99** *right* Linda Parham and David Slobham's apartment in Sydney designed by architect Stephen Varady; **100** *above* a house in Noosaville designed by John Mainwaring; **100** *below* Stephen Woodham's house in London designed in conjunction with Mark Brook Design; **101** Paula Pryke and Peter Romaniuk's house in London; **102–3** Mike and Kris Taylor's loft in London designed by Circus Architects with Kayode Lipede; **103** *below* designed by Interni Interior Design Consultancy; **104** a house in Sydney designed by Larcombe and Solomon; **106** an apartment in Paris designed by Hervé Vermesch; **107** Consuelo Zoelly's apartment in Paris; **108–9** a kitchen in London designed by Rick Baker; **110** Felix Bonnier's apartment in Paris; **111** *above left and above center* kitchen by Rhode Design; **111** *above right* kitchen by Chalon; **111** *center and center right* a house in London designed by Amanda Hannam of W.H. Designs; **111** *below right* Patricia Wong's apartment in New York designed by Amanda Halstead; **113** *above* a kitchen in London designed by Rick Baker; **113** *below* Paula Pryke and Peter Romaniuk's house in London; **114** *below right* a kitchen in London designed by Rick Baker; **117** *below* Christine Walsh and Ian Bartlett's house in London designed by Jack Ingham of Bookworks; **118** *above right* Douglas and Dorothy Hamilton's apartment in New York; **119** Consuelo Zoelly's apartment in Paris; **122** *left* Charles Mount Morris and Harold Gordon's house on Long Island designed by Charles Morris Mount/stove by U.S. Range; **122** *right* Felix Bonnier's apartment in Paris; **123** Felix Bonnier's apartment in Paris; **124** Victor Ktori's loft in London designed by Circus Architects; **124–25** an apartment in Paris designed by Hervé Vermesch; **126** Amanda and Andrew Manning's house in Melbourne designed by architect Stephen Varady; **128** *above left* Dominique Lubar for IPL Interiors; **128** *above center and above right* Melvyn Gadsdon's loft in London/kitchen by Bulthaup; **131** *center right* Grant Ford and Jane Bailey's house in London/kitchen by Rhode Design; **133** Linda Parham and David Slobham's apartment in Sydney designed by architect Stephen Varady; **135** *above left* kitchen by Bulthaup; **137** *left* Sally Butler's house in London; **137** *above right* a house in London designed by Amanda Hannam of W.H. Designs; **139** *above and center right* an apartment in New York designed by Marino & Giolito; **139** *center left* Suzanne Slesin and Michael Steinberg's apartment in New York designed by architect Jean-Louis Ménard; **140** *above and below right* Stephen Woodham's house in London designed in conjunction with Mark Brook Design; **140** *below left and below center* Gale Edwards' apartment in London designed by Hester Gray; **141** Paula Pryke and Peter Romaniuk's house in London; **142** *above* Christine Walsh and Ian Bartlett's house in London designed by Jack Ingham of Bookworks; **143** an apartment in Paris designed by Hervé Vermesch ; **144** *above* Grant Ford and Jane Bailey's house in London/kitchen by Rhode Design; **144** *below* Nigel Rowe's house in Middlesex/kitchen by Crabtree Kitchens; **145** Grant Ford and Jane Bailey's house in London/kitchen by Rhode Design; **146–47** a house in London designed by stylist Baba Bolli/kitchen by Smallbone; **148–49** Mike and Kris Taylor's loft in London designed by Circus Architects with Kayode Lipede; **150** *above* Linda Parham and David Slobham's apartment in Sydney designed by architect Stephen Varady; **150** *below* Andrew Arnott and Karin Schack's house in Melbourne; **152** *above* Consuelo Zoelly's apartment in Paris; **152** *below* an apartment in Paris designed by Hervé Vermesch ; **152–53** Consuelo Zoelly's apartment in Paris; **154** *center left* Charles Morris Mount and Harold Gordon's house on Long Island designed by Charles Morris Mount; **154** *below right* Gale Edwards' apartment in London designed by Hester Gray; **154** *below left* designed by Interni Interior Design Consultancy; **155** *above* Victor Ktori's loft in London designed by Circus Arcitects; **155** *below* Gale Edwards' apartment in London designed by Hester Gray; **157** *above* an apartment in New York designed by Marino & Giolito; **159** designed by Interni Interior Design Consultancy; **160** *above* Suzanne Slesin and Michael Steinberg's apartment in New York designed by architect Jean-Louis Ménard; **160** *below left* Consuelo Zoelly's apartment in Paris; **161** *below right* the Ash house in London designed by Ash Sakula Architects; **162–63** Vicky and Simon Young's house in Northumberland; **164** a kitchen in London designed by Rick Baker; **166–67** Sally Butler's house in London; **168–69** Vicky and Simon Young's house in Northumberland; **170** a house in Queensland designed by Tony Suttle; **171** *above right* Amanda and Andrew Manning's apartment in Sydney designed by architect Stephen Varady; **171** *below* Janick and Hubert Schoumacher-Vilfroy's house in Normandy; **172** *left* a kitchen in London designed by Rick Baker; **172** *right* an apartment in London designed by Ash Sakula Architects; **173** an apartment in London designed by Ash Sakula Architects; **174–75** Sophie Sarin's apartment in London; **176** Suzanne Slesin and Michael Steinberg's apartment in New York designed by architect Jean-Louis Ménard; **177** *left* a house in Sydney designed by Luigi Roselli; **177** *right* Charles Morris Mount and Harold Gordon's house on Long Island designed by Charles Morris Mount/flooring by Formica® Corporation; **178** *above left* Victor Ktori's loft in London designed by Circus Architects; **178** *above right* Jan Staller's apartment in New York; **178** *below* an apartment in New York designed by Marino & Giolito; **179** Christine Walsh and Ian Bartlett's house in London designed by Jack Ingham of Bookworks; **180** the Ash house in London designed by Ash Sakula Architects; **181** *above left* Melvyn Gadsdon's loft in London; **181** *below* an apartment in Paris designed by Hervé Vermesch.

Author's Acknowledgments

Many thanks to **Lillian O'Bourke** of New Hearth, New York, for her help and many introductions. **Tim Boyd** of Delia Associates, New Haven, for his time and assistance. Also to **Anna Hickman, Shelia Fitzjones, Gill Sheppard,** and **Janet Kennedy** in tracking down locations and especially to the team at **Ryland, Peters & Small—Sian** for her excellent forward planning and **Anne** and **Jacqui** for their support.

index